CAMPAIGN 324

CAMPALDINO 1289

The battle that made Dante

KELLY DEVRIES AND NICCOLÒ CAPPONI

ILLUSTRATED BY GRAHAM TURNER

Series Editor Marcus Cowper

OSPREY
Bloomsbury Publishing Plc
PO Box 883, Oxford, OX1 9PL, UK
1385 Broadway, 5th Floor, New York, NY 10018, USA
E-mail: info@ospreypublishing.com
www.ospreypublishing.com

OSPREY is a trademark of Osprey Publishing Ltd

First published in Great Britain in 2018

A catalog record for this book is available from the British Library.

ISBN: PB 9781472831286; eBook 9781472831279; ePDF 9781472831262;
XML 9781472831255

18 19 20 21 22 10 9 8 7 6 5 4 3 2 1

Maps by Bounford.com
3D BEVs by The Black Spot
Index by Alan Rutter
Typeset by PDQ Digital Media Solutions, Bungay, UK
Printed in China through World Print Ltd

DEDICATION

For Tessa, since the Cerchi blood is much thicker than water.

ACKNOWLEDGMENTS

The authors would like to thank the following who helped with the
preparation of this book: Robert Woosnam-Savage of the Royal Armouries;
Michael Livingston of The Citadel; Dr Fulvio Silvano Stacchetti and the staff
of the Biblioteca Riccardiana, Florence; Dr Silvia Alessandri; Dr Francesca
Klein; Dr Silvia Castelli; Professor Ugo Barlozzetti; Professor Franco Cardini;
Francesca Capponi; Dr Ilaria Ciseri; Dr Mary V. Davidson; Dr Graziano
Raveggi; Dr Antonella Nesi and the staff of the Museo Stefano Bardini,
Florence; Umiliana de' Cerchi; Mr Vasco Goretti, for access to the church of
Certomondo; and Maria Pertile – for putting up with two military historians.

ARTIST'S NOTE

Readers may care to note that the original paintings from which the color
plates in this book were prepared are available for private sale. All
reproduction copyright whatsoever is retained by the publishers. All
enquiries should be addressed to:

Graham Turner, PO Box 568, Aylesbury, Bucks, HP17 8EX, UK
www.studio88.co.uk

The publishers regret that they can enter into no correspondence upon
this matter.

Osprey Publishing supports the Woodland Trust, the UK's leading woodland
conservation charity. Between 2014 and 2018 our donations are being
spent on their Centenary Woods project in the UK.

To find out more about our authors and books, visit
www.ospreypublishing.com. Here you will find extracts, author
interviews, details of forthcoming events and the option to sign up for
our newsletter.

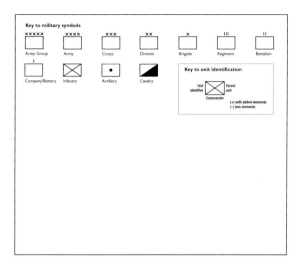

CONTENTS

Italy in the late 13th century

Legend:
- Guelphs
- Ghibellines
- Other/not applicable

FRIULI

LOMBARDY
Como · Bergamo · Brescia · Novara · Milan · Vercelli · Pavia · Turin · Asti · Alessandria · Piacenza · Cremona · Mantua · Vicenza · Treviso · Verona · Padua · Venice

PIEDMONT

EMILIA
Parma · Modena · Reggio · Bologna · Imola · Ferrara · Ravenna · Faenza · Forlì · Genoa

ROMAGNA
Rimini · Urbino · Fano

Pistoia · Lucca · Prato · Pisa · Florence · Volterra · Arezzo · Siena · Gubbio · Ancona

MARCHE

TUSCANY
Orvieto · Perugia · Spoleto · Viterbo

UMBRIA

LATIUM
Rome

ABRUZZO
L'Aquila

MOLISE

CAMPANIA
Lucera · Naples · Salerno · Amalfi

APULIA
Brindisi

BASILICATA

CORSICA
(Genoa)

SARDINIA
(Pisa and
independent polities)

KINGDOM OF NAPLES
(Angevins)

CALABRIA

Palermo · Reggio

KINGDOM OF SICILY
(Aragonese)

0 — 100 miles
0 — 100km

N

INTRODUCTION

Many a score was settled on the blood-soaked field below the castle of Poppi on 11 June 1289, personal animosities inextricably entwined with factional rivalry. For over seven decades Tuscany – and Italy, for that matter – had been plagued by internecine strife between the Guelphs – backing Papal political power – and the Ghibellines – supporting Holy Roman imperial power. However, after the death of Emperor Frederick II in 1250 these clear-cut distinctions had become blurred, and a state's adherence to one of the two factions was dictated as much by the ideology of its ruling group as by broader political motivations, with the two factors frequently conflicting. Thus, in 1260 Guelph Florence would fight Ghibelline Siena in the name of the imperial claimant Conradin of Swabia – and while under Papal interdict! The conquest of southern Italy by Charles of Anjou in 1266 produced a substantial reshuffling of Italian politics, with Guelphism now identified with Angevin rule. Florentine merchants and bankers, amongst others, hugely benefitted from the new settlement and Ghibellinism, to them, was not just an ideological opposite, but also potentially damaging economically. The rise of new champions of the Ghibelline cause in the early 1280s, such as the kings of Aragon and the Montefeltro family, caused increasing alarm in the Guelph states of central Italy and led down a road that would end on the field of Campaldino.

Some battles are famous because of their historical impact; others because of their literary significance. In the case of Campaldino, its importance as an event is dwarfed in the common imagery by its poetic description in Dante Alighieri's *Divine Comedy*. In the fifth canto of *Purgatory*, Dante's encounter with the shade of one of those vanquished in the battle leads, in a dramatic crescendo, to one of the most celebrated passages in the whole poem. Commentators old and recent have made much of this vignette, also pointing out the other moments in the poem in which Dante makes a direct, and sometimes indirect, reference to the campaign of 1289. Yet, something appears to be missing from these otherwise fine pieces of scholarly criticism.

The fact is that the whole of the *Divine Comedy* hinges in one way or other on Campaldino, the blood-splashed Saturday morning fixated in Dante's mind, both as one of the participants and for the battle's long-term consequences that affected directly the Florentine poet's destiny. Dante himself would bluntly state as much, in a letter, written probably during his exile from his native city, and surviving only in a 15th-century fragment copied by the humanist Leonardo Bruni:

All the evil and inconveniences that befell me from the beginning of my Priorate were caused and commenced from that office, of which I was unworthy due to prudence alone, not because of age and commitment; for ten years had already elapsed since the battle of Campaldino, in which the Ghibelline party was almost utterly defeated and effaced, where I found myself no youngster in the practice of arms, and where at the beginning I felt great fear, and in the end even greater joy through the varying fortunes of that fight.

Campaldino and, one can solidly speculate, the horrors of hand-to-hand fighting, shaped Dante in no uncertain ways, bringing the somewhat rarefied poet face-to-face with the solid brutality of combat. What the part-time Florentine soldier saw would seep into a masterpiece of the ages, making the *Divine Comedy* not just a unique poetic composition, but also a too often disregarded historical document on the reality of medieval warfare. Indeed, Dante's battlefield experience is often reflected in the suffering inflicted on the dammed in the *Inferno*: dismemberment by edged weapons, submersion in blood, naked under lashing rain, and so on. In one semi-comedic moment, Dante compares the devils escorting him to an army on the march, immediately afterwards recalling his raiding experiences during the campaign of 1289. It has been said by a few commentators that the Florentine poet may have been subjected to epileptic fits, due to his self-recorded tendency to swoon; at the risk of sounding anachronistic, from evidence in his writings it is equally possible that he suffered from a form of PTSD, induced by the brutal brush with widespread killing.

Still, Campaldino as an historical event has a life of its own outside the *Divine Comedy*. For Florence, it represented not only a military success but also a psychological one, the Guelph regime proving it could hold its own against external foes, while playing a hegemonic role within the Tuscan anti-Ghibelline league. Besides, from a strictly strategic angle, the battle delivered what the Guelphs had been seeking, although the clash was in no way decisive in the modern sense. In the long run, it would lead to another encounter, in which Dante would be once more a protagonist and this time among the vanquished.

Dante Alighieri. One of the earliest portraits of Dante comes from a fresco by Giotto in the Palazzo del Bargello, Florence. The gentleness of the poet's features fits well with the pathos time and time again expressed in the *Divine Comedy*, which belies Dante's steely determination when hounding in verse those he despised. (Photo by Art Media/Print Collector/Getty Images)

THE STRATEGIC BACKGROUND

At the beginning of 1282, the king of Naples, Charles I of Anjou – 'he of the virile nose' as Dante, a master of one-liners, pointedly described him – was the most powerful sovereign in the Mediterranean. His domains stretched from Anjou to southern Italy, the kingdoms of Naples and Sicily acquired on the battlefield by defeating Manfred of Sicily at Benevento in 1266 and Conradin of Swabia at Tagliacozzo two years later. Backed by Pope Martin IV, Charles' military power threatened to extend into the rest of Italy, and this had allowed the Guelph faction to take over many of the states of north and central Italy, ousting the Ghibellines. In Tuscany, Florence had become a stronghold of Guelphism – the city's bankers especially benefitting from the Papal-Angevin alliance – with the other city-states of the region, Pisa excluded, following its example, to a greater or lesser degree, soon afterward.

Charles and the Guelphs had risen also because of the absence of an Imperial presence in Italy. Following the death of Frederick II in 1250, various pretenders claimed the Imperial throne. This chaotic situation ended only in 1274 with the election of Rudolf of Habsburg as King of the Romans (later Emperor Rudolf I) and his victory four years later at the battle of Marchfeld over the rival claimant Ottokar II of Bohemia. Rudolf's rise gave new strength to the Italian Ghibellines, with Milan falling under the sway of the Imperialist Visconti family in 1277 and many of the lords of northern and central Italy able once again to openly declare their fealty to the Empire. Worse was to come for the Guelph cause in the Italian peninsula. On 31 March 1282, an anti-Angevin conspiracy with international ramifications caused an uprising in Palermo (the famous 'Sicilian Vespers'), that swiftly snowballed into a general revolt engulfing the whole of Sicily and forcing Charles to shelve plans to expand into the Eastern Mediterranean against Constantinople. The Sicilians would eventually choose as their king Pedro III of Aragon, who had married Manfred of Swabia's daughter. Pedro would become the Ghibellines' main champion.

Ghibelline leaders responded quickly. On 1 May 1282, an army led by Guido di Montefeltro, a powerful lord of the Romagna area, annihilated a joint Angevin-Papal force outside Forlì – 'the bloody pile of Frenchmen,' as Dante would put it – while Buonconte di Montefeltro, Guido's son, together with Conrad of Swabia, grandson of Frederick II, created serious disturbances in the Papal territories of central Italy. Charles of Anjou fared poorly during the early years of the Wars of the Sicilian Vespers. Rebuffed in his attempts to retake Sicily, he suffered a series of defeats at sea, with

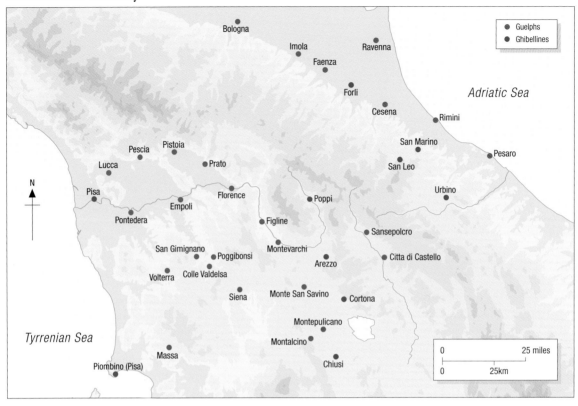

his own son and heir, Charles 'the lame,' (later Charles II) captured by the Aragonese in 1284 after a naval engagement off the coast of Naples.

TUSCAN MEDLEY

All these events were followed with apprehension in Florence, the Florentines on one hand worried about the loss of Angevin protection, and on the other not totally displeased that Charles' looming shadow over the city was diminished. This was especially felt by the *popolo* (tax-paying merchants and artisans), resentful that Charles during his exceptionally long tenure as *podestà* (a non-native appointed chief executive) had, through his representatives, favoured the city's aristocracy (the so-called magnates). The return of many Ghibellines from exile in 1280 increased the Florentine *popolo*'s concerns, believing that this meant a strengthening of the nobility. Significantly, four months after the outburst of the Sicilian Vespers, the city's guilds managed to put in place a governmental advisory body, the *Priorate*, that within a year had become Florence's executive magistracy. However, rather than oppose this new institutional body, the magnates, through their power and influence, attempted to take it over, many signing themselves up as guildsmen and thus continuing to dominate Florentine politics.

Widespread factional strife did not erupt in Florence only because international situations forced its citizens to bond together – albeit after a fashion – against external foes. In late autumn of 1284, Florence, Lucca,

Genoa and a number of Tuscan states formed a league against Pisa, exploiting the Pisans' weakness after the disastrous naval defeat they had suffered at Meloria earlier that year at the hands of the Genoese (the regimes of Genoa and Pisa were both Ghibelline, but commercial rivalries in the eastern Mediterranean proved stronger than political factionalism). For the Florentines, and the Guelphs in general, the Pisa campaign proved successful. Pressed on all sides, the Pisans were forced to cede a sizeable number of important strongholds and, in an attempt to forestall the impending doom, hand over the reins of government to the staunchly Guelph Ugolino della Gherardesca, count of Donoratico. At this point, having obtained most of its goals, Florence let the military situation stagnate. Also, somewhat hypocritically, the Florentines eagerly accepted papal mediation to end the conflict which, together with Lucca leaving the league in the summer of 1285, left the Genoese to fend for themselves. The loss of Pisa was a serious blow for the Ghibellines, compounded also by Guido di Montefeltro being ousted from his holdings in the Romagna region by a papal army and a pro-Guelph insurrection. The Ghibelline leader was exiled to Piedmont after submitting to the pope.

Despite all these successes, the international situation did not bode well for the Guelphs. In January 1285 Charles of Anjou died, and two months later Pope Martin IV, a committed Angevin ally, also went to his grave. The new pope, Honorius IV, while adamant in upholding the Angevin cause against the Aragonese, showed equal commitment in pursuing a peaceful settlement regarding the Sicilian question. Furthermore, a massive French expedition against Pedro in Catalonia stalled in front of Girona and was eventually forced to retreat, while, once again, the Aragonese dominated at sea. Luckily for the Guelphs, Pedro passed away in November, but with the new king of Naples still a prisoner in Aragon, the Angevin cause appeared in jeopardy.

In Tuscany the Ghibelline presence was being felt, despite the loss of Pisa. The lords of the upper Arno Valley, in particular the Pazzi and the Ubertini, had been creating disturbances, their actions threatening to sever the communication routes from Florence to the south and cause political upheavals in Arezzo. Arezzo was ruled by a local *popolo*, and therefore the Florentine magnates were more concerned in helping the Aretine nobility than stemming the Ghibelline tide. As a result, Florence was slow to react, counting also on the fact that Arezzo's *podestà* happened to be a Florentine. Therefore, it came as a rude shock when Guglielmino degli Ubertini, bishop of Arezzo, allied himself with the local *popolo* to evict the *podestà* in the spring of 1285. As a consequence, the city soon became a haven for exiled Tuscan Ghibellines, leading to further trouble in the region.

This fresco by Giotto, dated *c*.1295, depicts St Francis of Assisi and his follower Sylvester of Assisi evicting the devils from Arezzo. The tall, cramped, multi-coloured buildings depicted here could be seen in any city or town of central Italy, with the colour combinations shown on plastered walls often identifying different neighbourhoods. Whether by chance or design, Giotto underscores the running tensions between Arezzo and its bishops by giving prominence to the old cathedral, standing well outside the city's walls. (The Expulsion of the Devils from Arezzo, 1297–99 (fresco), Giotto di Bondone (*c*.1266–1337)/ San Francesco, Upper Church, Assisi, Italy/Bridgeman Images)

Siena was regarded as the soft underbelly of the 'Guelph League' (*Taglia Guelfa*), an alliance comprising the cities of Florence, Lucca, Pistoia, Prato, Siena and Volterra. In the 1260s Siena had been staunchly Imperialist. On 4 September 1260 the Sienese aided by Manfred of Swabia's forces and exiled Florentine Ghibellines won the great victory at Montaperti against a Guelph coalition under Florence's leadership – 'the day the river Arbia ran red', to use Dante's words. The end of Manfred's power in 1266 also meant the downfall of Ghibellinism in Siena, the Sienese being defeated in 1269 at Colle Val d'Elsa by a joint Florentine-Angevin force. Siena, therefore, was forced to bow to Charles of Anjou and accept a Guelph regime. Still, the Sienese nobility remained lukewarm at best about these changes, in particular as the city was now under the sway of the local *popolo*. The Guelphs rightly feared that an attack against Siena could trigger a political revolution, causing a return to power of the Ghibellines.

This attack materialized in September 1285, when a group of Sienese and Florentine exiles seized the castle of Poggio Santa Cecilia some 20 miles east of Siena, threatening a number of important roads. Siena and Florence this time acted swiftly, and by the end of October the castle was under siege by a Guelph force, including Pisan knights sent by Count Ugolino, led by the redoubtable Guy de Monfort. The besieged were hoping the bishop of Arezzo, Guglielmino degli Ubertini, would come to their aid, but he preferred to play a waiting game, reckoning that the siege would commit his Guelph foes long enough to allow the Ghibellines to build up their strength. Eventually, on the night of 6–7 April 1286, having been reduced to eating rats and drinking their own urine, some of the defenders of Poggio Santa Cecilia attempted to escape. A few managed, but others were captured and thrown into Florentine prisons where they languished for decades. The fate of those left in the castle was rather more savage once they surrendered: hanged by the dozen along the Arbia River or beheaded in Siena's main square. Ubertini himself came to terms the following August, after his forces were mauled by the Guelphs in the field; in return for peace, he agreed to expel the Ghibelline exiles from Arezzo.

Ubertini's apparent subservience was simply a ruse to gain time, however. Despite the debacle of Poggio Santa Cecilia, the Ghibellines now had received an unexpected boost. July 1286 had seen the arrival in Tuscany of Percivalle Fieschi, Imperial Vicar and prelate. Rudolf of Habsburg's choice for his representative may seem strange, considering Fieschi's proximity to Charles of Anjou; he also happened to be the nephew of one previous pope, Innocent IV, and the brother of another, Adrian V. But he was also related to Rudolf by marriage, besides the fact that his mission was part of a concerted plan between the pope and the emperor-elect concerning their respective spheres of influence in Italy. At the time of his election as King of the Romans, in order to gain the pope's support, Rudolf renounced his rights over the Romagna in the papacy's favour (although some argued that an emperor-elect had no right to do such a thing) and now intended to do the same with Tuscany to assure the succession of his son, Albert. Significantly, and in a stark reversal of the papacy's pro-Guelph policy, Honorius sent a message to the Florentines ordering them to obey the Imperial Vicar's orders.

Fieschi held a *parlamento* (general assembly) of all Tuscan political entities on 21 July 1286 in the town of San Miniato, the ancient seat of Imperial authority in Tuscany, during which he demanded that the states of the region swear allegiance to Rudolf and cede to him all the rights of Imperial origin that they might possess. The Florentines protested against what they considered an abuse of power, while Siena tried to appease the Vicar with vague promises and a generous monetary gift. Unimpressed, Fieschi imposed on Florence a fine of 50,000 silver marks (£25,000) and on Siena one of 30,000 (£15,000), declaring the credits and goods owned by merchants of the two cities within the Empire collaterals to the payment. Florence and Siena shrugged off these utterances, since Fieschi had no military force to back them.

Matters became somewhat more worrisome for the Guelphs when the Vicar decided to move to Arezzo as Ubertini's guest. Even more alarming proved the news that Rudolf intended a descent into Italy the following year to be crowned in Rome on Candlemass 1287. Honorius' ailing condition forced the emperor-elect to postpone his Italian adventure – indefinitely, as it turned out, as Honorius died in April 1287. The vacancy of the Holy See compelled Prencivalle to return to Germany until the following year in order to consult with Rudolf. In March 1287, delegates of the Tuscan Guelph cities gathered in Castelfiorentino, where they agreed on a new league to oppose the King of the Romans' (and, indirectly, the pope's) future actions with a force of 1,500 citizen and 500 mercenary cavalry under the alliance's new military leader, the experienced fighter Ranuccio Farnese.

These decisions came just before a major political crisis erupted in Arezzo. The Aretine leader of the local guilds was one Guelfo da Lombrici, from Lucca, and in the spring of 1287 he organized a popular uprising which led to the eviction of the city's nobility, Guelph and Ghibelline, as well as Bishop Ubertini. The following June they managed to retake Arezzo with a surprise attack, capturing and executing Lombrici and destroying the power of the *popolo*. In August the Ghibellines evicted the Guelphs after a fierce struggle, thanks to the *masnade* (retainers) of the Ubertini, the Pazzi, the Guidi of Poppi and the aid of Buonconte di Montefeltro, who was considered at the time to have masterminded the operation.

The news coming from Arezzo was ill received in Florence, the Florentines immediately bestowing emergency powers on the government to protect the city and other allied states from the renewed Ghibelline threat. The possibility of a conflict had, at least, the beneficial consequence of ending a spat of domestic political violence that had plagued the city during the previous months, mainly caused by the lawlessness of some aristocrats, in particular the firebrand Corso Donati. The Guelphs had reasons for concern, since they could not count on any support from the vacant papacy, while the Angevins in the south had their hands full after suffering yet another naval defeat to the Aragonese, losing several important leaders killed or captured, including Guy de Montfort. To add to their woes, in the late autumn Percivalle Fieschi returned to Tuscany, this time with a military retinue, taking up residence in Arezzo. A Guelph-Ghibelline conflict was now inevitable, and the only uncertainty was who would strike first.

A keep surrounded by a wooden fortification. Wooden walls were common in many places throughout Europe during the 13th century. (Photo by Sergio Anelli/Electa/Mondadori Portfolio via Getty Images)

Military operations, 1288–89

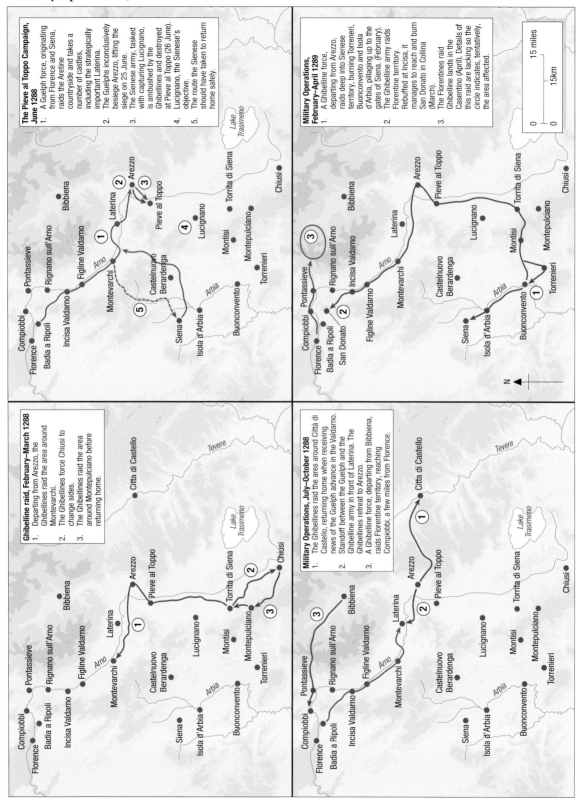

The Pieve al Toppo Campaign, June 1288

1. A Guelph force, originating from Florence and Siena, raids the Aretine countryside and takes a number of castles, including the strategically important Laterina.
2. The Guelphs inconclusively besiege Arezzo, lifting the siege on 25 June.
3. The Sienese army, tasked with capturing Lucignano, is ambushed by the Ghibellines and destroyed at Pieve al Toppo (26 June). Lucignano, the Sienese's objective.
4.
5. The route the Sienese should have taken to return home safely.

Military Operations, February–April 1289

1. A Ghibelline force, departing from Arezzo, raids deep into Sienese territory, burning Torreneri, Buonconvento and Isola d'Arbia, pillaging up to the gates of Siena. (February).
2. The Ghibelline army raids Florentine territory. Rebuffed at Incisa, it manages to reach and burn San Donato in Collina (March).
3. The Florentines raid Ghibelline lands in the Casentino (April). Details of this raid are lacking so the circle indicates, tentatively, the area affected.

0   15 miles

0   15km

Ghibelline raid, February–March 1288

1. Departing from Arezzo, the Ghibellines raid the area around Montevarchi.
2. The Ghibellines force Chiusi to change sides.
3. The Ghibellines raid the area around Montepulciano before returning home.

Military Operations, July–October 1288

1. The Ghibellines raid the area around Citta di Castello, returning home when receiving news of the Guelph advance in the Valdarno.
2. Standoff between the Guelph and the Ghibelline army in front of Laterina. The Ghibellines retreat to Arezzo.
3. A Ghibelline force, departing from Bibbiena, raids Florentine territory, reaching Compiobbi, a few miles from Florence.

JOUSTS AND STARVATION

In February 1288 the Ghibellines were the first to take the field, invading Florentine territory, laying waste to the area around Montevarchi and forcing the Guelphs on the defensive. The Imperialists then moved on to Chiusi, left undefended by the Sienese, and compelled the town to side with them. The Ghibellines were also favoured by the policies of the new pope, Nicholas IV. Elected nearly a year after his predecessor's death, Nicholas tried to bring the warring parties to the negotiation table, threatening to excommunicate all who refused to comply. Showing himself a dutiful son of the Church, Fieschi went in person to negotiate with the pope, then in Rieti, while at the same time rallying to his banner the Ghibellines from Tuscany, the Romagna, the Duchy of Spoleto and the March of Ancona. The Florentines and the Sienese simply ignored the pontiff's threats – despite some formal and hypocritical hand-wringing – and continued their military build up.

On 1 June a 15,000-strong Guelph host, including contingents from Bologna and the Romagna, entered Aretine territory from the north-east and the south-east, in rapid succession occupying several castles in the upper Arno Valley and in the Val d'Ambra, some of which were razed and others garrisoned. The now-united invading army proceeded to lay siege to Arezzo itself, but, lacking the necessary equipment, could do little except devastate the surrounding countryside. On 24 June, the feast of St John the Baptist, Florence's patron saint, the Florentines ran a *palio* (horse race) under the walls of the city and in full view of the besieged dubbed 12 young men as knights. Having completed these shows of bravado the Guelphs struck camp the next day, heading for home feeling thoroughly satisfied. Smugness, however, often comes at a hefty price.

Instead of marching to Montevarchi, into the Chianti and then south to return home, the Sienese contingent, comprising 3,000 foot and 600–700 horse under their *podestà* Guido Salvatico Guidi (the Guidi were divided in their political allegiances) and Ranuccio Farnese, took the road to the Val di Chiana in order to attack the rebellious and strategically important castle of Lucignano, midway between Arezzo and Siena. Whether through intelligence or because they guessed the Sienese objectives correctly, the Ghibelline commanders, Buonconte di Montefeltro and Guglielmo de' Pazzi, gathered a force of 300 horse and 2,000 select infantry. Half of the latter they dispatched to shadow the Sienese, while the rest of the army marched under the cover of darkness by a circuitous route to the Chiana River near Pieve al Toppo, a nearby ford and a path across the valley's marshy ground. The Sienese appeared on the morning of the 26th in good order but totally unprepared: the crossbowmen's pavises were with the baggage train together with the knights' lances, while the horsemen had their shields tied to the saddles.

No sooner had the Sienese started crossing the ford, than Buonconte and Guglielmo sprang their trap. From among the nearby reeds and bushes came a hail of bolts that hit the advancing army squarely in the flank. As the Guelphs desperately tried to deploy, the Ghibelline cavalry smashed into their disarrayed ranks. The fight quickly turned into a shambles as the Guelph array fragmented into small groups, some of them fleeing, with others trying to put up some sort of resistance. These fights, reminiscent of a tournament, caused the clash to be dubbed 'the Jousts of Toppo' – Dante mockingly using the phrase when meeting in Hell among the profligates a Sienese victim of

The battlefield of Pieve al Toppo, where Ghibelline troops trapped and easily defeated Guelph soldiers, primarily Sienese militia with a few score mercenary cavalry on 26 June 1288. (Authors' Collection)

the battle, whose legs had not been 'fast enough' on that day. Those Guelphs blessed with speed managed to flee from the carnage; many others were not so lucky, being hunted down by the victorious Ghibellines and the local peasantry. Roughly 300 cavalrymen, mostly Sienese, lay dead on the field, while another 200 horsemen and an unspecified number of infantry were taken prisoners. The slain included Farnese, while Guido Salvatico made good his escape to Siena.

As the Guelph states rushed through emergency measures in the immediate aftermath of the debacle, they were hit by a disaster of even greater magnitude. In Pisa Count Ugolino's regime had become increasingly unpopular due to its inability to counter the Genoese threat to Pisa's maritime trade. Peace negotiations with Genoa had been proceeding with difficulty, because of the Genoese demands, and in the meantime the Ghibellines in the city, headed by the Archbishop Ruggieri degli Ubaldini, were plotting a regime change, confident that the majority of the populace opposed the Guelph government. On 30 June a 'spontaneous' uprising in Pisa left Ugolino isolated, and soon after he was captured together with a number of his kinsmen. Ruggieri proclaimed himself *podestà*, expelled the Guelphs from the city and had the Count and his relatives – with the exception of one still a baby – locked up in a tower. In the following months, the prelate fleeced his prisoners of their money, and, when they could pay no longer, left them to starve to death. Dante would later place both Ugolino and Ruggieri in Hell among the traitors, the count gnawing the archbishop's skull for all eternity.

The loss of Pisa opened another front for the Guelphs, forcing Florence and Lucca to send men and resources against the new threat. Luckily, the Pisan exiles were led by the resolute Nino Visconti, Ugolino's grandson, who together with Lucca's forces pursued an aggressive campaign and kept the Pisans at bay. On the Aretine front, the Ghibellines, in high spirits after the victory at Pieve al Toppo, had taken the war into Umbria and ransacked the area around Città di Castello. To relieve the pressure on the Umbrian Guelphs, in mid-September Florence hurriedly despatched a raiding force 5,000 strong into Aretine territory. The Ghibellines rushed back to Arezzo and from there sent their foes a formal challenge to battle. A few days later

the two armies – the Ghibellines with the advantage of numbers – faced each other across the Arno near Laterina, which the Florentines had captured two months back. The Guelphs proposed that the Ghibellines cross the shallow waters or, alternatively, allowed the Guelphs to cross the river and deploy on the opposite side. The Ghibellines, however, refused both options, believing their adversaries to be planning some trick, and made their way back to Arezzo. The Guelphs claimed a moral victory, and underscored it by taking a number of castles in the area. To save face, the Ghibellines launched a raid in the Val di Sieve from the Casentino, leaving a trail of destruction up to the village of Compiobbi, less than six miles from Florence's walls. Both armies then retired to winter quarters.

The effects of raiding as shown in a fresco, *Bad Government*, painted by Ambrogio Lorenzetti c.1330, on the wall of the Palazzo Pubblico, Siena. Ruined castles, torched hamlets and barren fields litter the countryside, populated only by the shadowy figures of soldiers, veritable fiends from Hell for the victimized populace. (Photo by Antonio Quattrone/Archivio Antonio Quattrone/Mondadori Portfolio via Getty Images)

All considered, 1288 belonged to the Ghibellines. Despite some territorial losses, they had won a major battle, caused a regime change in Pisa and most of the time held the military upper hand. For the beleaguered Guelphs, the last months of the year carried some good tidings. On 29 October, Charles II of Naples obtained his freedom, thanks to Edward I of England's mediation, a few concessions to his captors and a hefty ransom, a substantial chunk of which the Florentines agreed to pay. It was money well spent, for now the Guelphs could count on the active political and military support of the Neapolitan and, if less directly, the French crowns. Time was short for the Ghibellines, faced with the urgent need to consolidate their gains and enlarge their power base. Archbishop Ruggieri understood this when he sent an urgent message to the exiled Guido di Montefeltro in Piedmont, inviting one of the foremost Ghibelline leaders in Italy to become Pisa's political and military leader . It was not long before Guido, defying his inevitable excommunication, could be seen riding south towards Tuscany.

CHRONOLOGY

1282

31 March — The 'Sicilian Vespers' revolt against Charles I of Anjou, king of Naples, begins.

1 May — Franco-Papal army defeated at the battle of Forlì by the Ghibellines under Guido di Montefeltro.

August — Pedro II of Aragon elected king of Sicily.

1284

5 June — Charles, heir to the Neapolitan throne, captured by the Aragonese in a naval encounter.

6 August — Pisa defeated by Genoa in the battle of Meloria.

Autumn — Genoa, Lucca, Florence and other Tuscan states form an anti-Pisan league.

1285

7 January — Death of Charles of Anjou; his son, still a prisoner in Aragon, becomes Charles II of Naples.

February — The Guelph Count Ugolino della Gherardesca elected *podestà* of Pisa for ten years.

Summer — Guido di Montefeltro is forced to surrender to Pope Honorius IV and is exiled to Piedmont.

September — Ghibelline exiles from Siena and Florence capture the Sienese castle of Poggio Santa Cecilia.

10 November — Death of Pedro II of Aragon.

1286

April — Poggio Santa Cecilia is retaken by a Florentine-Sienese army after a lengthy siege.

July — Percivalle Fieschi, emperor-elect Rudolf of Habsburg's representative, arrives in Tuscany to reassert Imperial rights.

August — The cavalry of the bishop of Arezzo, Guglielmino degli Ubertini, is defeated by a Franco-Sienese force. Ubertini bows to Siena's requests to expel any Sienese Ghibelline exiles from his possessions.

1287

March — The Tuscan Guelph states form a league to oppose Rudolf's demands.

Spring — A popular rising in Arezzo evicts the local nobility, both Guelph and Ghibelline. In June, however, the aristocracy returns to the city, crushing the popular regime.

August — The Ghibelline nobles in Arezzo turn on their Guelph counterparts, evicting them from the city.

Autumn — Percivalle Fieschi takes up residence in Arezzo.

1288

February — Fieschi and the Aretines start hostilities by raiding Florentine territory and taking the Guelph town of Chiusi.

23 May — The Florentines raise their war standards at the Badia a Ripoli in the direction of Arezzo.

1–25 June — The Guelphs invade Aretine territory and lay siege to Arezzo, devastating the countryside. The inconclusive siege is lifted on 25 June.

26 June	The Sienese contingent returning from the siege of Arezzo is ambushed at Pieve al Toppo by the Ghibellines under Buonconte di Montefeltro and Guglielmo de' Pazzi, losing 300 knights and the commander of the Guelph League, Ranuccio Farnese.
30 June	A rising in Pisa, orchestrated by Archbishop Ruggieri degli Ubaldini, leads to the downfall of Count Ugolino, who is imprisoned in a tower with several kinsmen; eventually, all of them will be left to die of hunger.
September	In mid-month, the Florentines enter Aretine territory from their outpost of Laterina. A Ghibelline proposal for an arranged battle falls through because the two sides cannot agree on the battlefield.
13–14 October	To avenge the devastation of the Aretine countryside, the Ghibellines conduct a raid deep into Florentine territory, reaching Compiobbi, a few miles from Florence.
29 October	Charles II of Naples is freed from Aragonese captivity.

1289

1–13 March	The Ghibellines of Arezzo raid Sienese and Florentine territory.
15 March	Accepting Archbishop Ruggeri's invitation, Guido di Montefeltro arrives in Pisa after escaping his confinement in Piedmont.
April	The leaders of the Guelph league decide in favour of a general offensive against Arezzo.
May	Charles II of Naples arrives in Florence en route to be crowned by the pope in Rieti. He leaves behind 100 knights under Amauri de Narbonne and Guillaume de Durfort. Narbonne is created Captain-General of the Guelph

	league. In a meeting at the end of the month, they decide to attack Arezzo from the Casentino.
2 June	The Guelph army starts moving out of Florence. An advance party establishes a base at Monte al Pruno. Raids against Aretine territory are ruthlessly executed.
3–9 June	The rest of the Guelph host arrives at Monte al Pruno. The Ghibelline army, deployed to stop any inroads from the Valdarno, stages a forced march to counter the new threat.
10 June	In the morning, the Ghibelline army arrives in front of the castle of Poppi, taking up position on the plain of Campaldino. In the afternoon, the Guelph host descends into the valley, taking up position in front of the Ghibellines.
11 June	Battle of Campaldino.
12–19 June	In the wake of their victory, the Guelphs pillage the Aretine countryside, before laying siege to Arezzo.
June–July	An ineffectual siege is made by the Guelphs against Arezzo, which is abandoned in mid-July. The main war effort moves to the Pisa front.

1293

	After four years of inconclusive fighting, the Guelphs agree to peace with Pisa. With this comes an unofficial truce with Arezzo.

1302

	A split within the Florentine Guelphs leads to factional fighting and the exile of a number of citizens, including Dante Alighieri.

OPPOSING COMMANDERS

GUELPH COMMANDERS

Born around 1263, **Amauri de Narbonne** – son of Aimeri V, viscount of Narbonne – was considered by Florentine historians to be young and inexperienced at the time of Campaldino. This picture is somewhat misleading, since he had participated with his father in the frontier wars between France and Aragon, at one point being taken prisoner by King Pedro III and being held captive for several years until ransomed. During his imprisonment he probably came into contact with Charles II of Naples, also in Aragonese captivity, which would help to explain why he joined the freed Charles' retinue during his voyage to Italy in the spring of 1289. Amauri arrived in Florence just at the time the Guelphs were seeking a new Captain-General for their alliance: despite any shortcomings he may have possessed, Amauri could count on his own following of experienced and capable knights, as well as being Charles' *de facto* representative in Tuscany. In effect, he managed the 1289 campaign with competence, if not brilliance, although there were reservations about his military skills despite the victory at Campaldino. In a sonnet contemporary to the battle, the ribald Sienese poet Cecco Angiolieri addressed Dante Alighieri with a warning that women should not be taken in by the fake qualities of an unnamed 'Marshal', believed by many scholars to be Narbonne.

Guillaume Bernard de Durfort's fame rests mainly on his funerary monument in the Florentine church of the Santissima Annunziata. Contemporary documents and witnesses point to him as the real leader of the Guelph army at Campaldino, rather than the inexperienced Narbonne. However, we know tantalizingly little about Durfort, other that he served as Amauri's *balivus* (roughly deputy). It is possible he was born sometime in the 1240s and probably originated from the County of Foix; he certainly belonged to the bailiwick of Carcassone, where his family

possessed land. His last will and testament shows him to have been a pious man of some wealth, and he bequeathed his belongings, worth around 300 gold florins, to the Servite friars for the relief of the poor. The connection between Durfort and the Servites may have happened when the former had been in Florentine service in 1280, and it is therefore possible he spoke some Italian – a crucial factor when handling an army in which few spoke or understood Narbonne's southern French.

Brave, eloquent, generous, violent, arrogant and ruthless – **Corso Donati** had all of these characteristics in abundance. Born around 1250 in a powerful family, Corso was a demagogue and a man of action, never afraid to take the law into his own hands. In 1286 he was banished and fined for attempting to save a fellow magnate from the chopping block – although the man was eventually beheaded. In the Commune of Florence's councils, Corso always advocated extreme measures, legal or not, to protect Florentine interests. Yet he was considered an able administrator, holding a number of executive posts in various states, both in Tuscany and outside, and his skill as a military leader would be demonstrated during crucial moments at Campaldino.

'The Gate's Ass' – **Vieri de' Cerchi** was so dubbed by his political enemy Corso Donati, since the Cerchi had their houses in the Florentine *sesto* (district) of Saint Peter's Gate (*Porta San Piero*). The chronicler Dino Compagni described him as 'very good looking, but devoid of cunning and a bad speaker'. Vieri de' Cerchi, born sometime in the 1240s, owed his position in Florence to his family's immense wealth, which led him to adopt the trappings and behaviour of the city's nobility: something that was poorly received by his social superiors. Probably because of his fortune and level-headedness, he was chosen to lead the Guelph vanguard at Campaldino. This did not prove to be an inspired choice, though, and despite suffering from a bad leg, Vieri displayed great courage and determination during the battle.

Although not one of the named leaders at Campaldino, **Dante Alighieri** has been inextricably linked to the battle through his imagery of the conflict. A member of Florence's militia cavalry with aspirations of nobility, the 24-year-old Dante took his place in the Guelph vanguard. By his own admission, his performance deserved neither praise nor infamy. Nevertheless, his *Divine Comedy*, begun within a decade of the battle, constantly refers to episodes and words tied to Campaldino.

GHIBELLINE COMMANDERS

At a first glance, **Guglielmino degli Ubertini** would appear to fit the stereotypical worldly clergyman of literature. While there is no doubt that he often practised power mongering to a high degree in his more than 40 years as bishop of Arezzo (1248–89), switching his allegiance at will from Guelph to Ghibelline, he always had in mind the interests of his city and his diocese – at least when he saw them coinciding with his own and those of his family. A man of the sword as much as of the pen, at

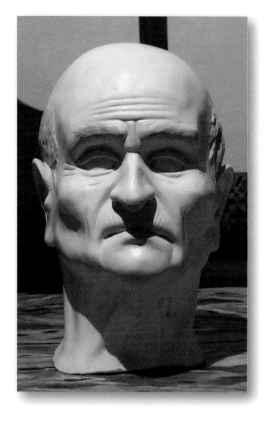

Bishop Guiglielmino degli Ubertini was killed at Campaldino and his bones interred under the nave of the church of Certomondo. However, in 2008 his skeleton was identified by DNA, exhumed and reinterred in Arezzo Cathedral. At the time this forensic reconstruction was sculpted based on his skull. (Authors' Collection)

the battle of Montaperti in 1260 Ubertini led the exiled Aretine Ghibellines against the Guelph coalition besieging Siena 'capturing and killing many'. On a number of occasions he did not hesitate to use the weapon of ecclesiastical censure against his fellow citizens to obtain his political goals. As a military leader he would show his limits during the 1289 campaign, when concerns over his own possessions in the Casentino area led him to seek battle at all costs, despite being advised otherwise. At Campaldino he demonstrated his attachment to his native city, not hesitating to join the fray even when given the chance to escape from the slaughter.

Buonconte di Montefeltro's name is bound to the battle of Campaldino, mostly because of Dante's imaginary meeting with him in Purgatory. Invention appears to have followed Buonconte in his afterlife and a later tradition has him being dubbed a knight by Rudolf of Habsburg in person (since the event is supposed to have happened in Perugia sometime in the mid-1280s when Rudolf was in Germany, we can well doubt its accuracy). The untimely death of Buonconte, probably still in his early 30s, undoubtedly contributed to the birth of legends around him, though his reputation as a strategist and tactician was well deserved. He had learned his trade through his father Guido; and although we cannot be certain he participated in the battle of Forlì in 1282, it may well be the case that he picked up a taste for ambushes there, together with an affinity for hit-and-run warfare. His waylaying of the Guelphs at Pieve al Toppo in 1288 was a brilliant operation, while on the day of Campaldino he advocated harassment tactics rather than facing the Guelph coalition in the field. The Ghibelline battle-plan at Campaldino clearly shows Buonconte's imprint and, if guilty of miscalculation, he erred only in believing the Florentine vanguard of better fighting quality than it proved in reality.

Having been the recognized leader of the Tuscan Ghibellines for nearly half a century before Campaldino, **Count Guido Novello Guidi** had all the traits of the survivor. A great admirer of St Francis of Assisi's mysticism, and yet a superstitious believer in astrology; the active political intriguer and the indolent chess-player; the brave leader of troops in battle and the living example of discretion (although some of his contemporaries would have defined it cowardice) being the best part of valour. In the course of his relatively long life he witnessed the waxing and waning of Ghibelline fortunes in Italy, taking part in many of the peninsula's key events. One of the Ghibelline commanders in the victorious battle of Montaperti (1260), he witnessed defeat at Tagliacozzo (1268) and at Colle Val d'Elsa (1269), saving his skin in the latter battles by timely retreats from the fray. Always an opportunist, his behaviour at Campaldino has been lambasted by Florentine (that is, Guelph) historians. Yet, in the long run his belief in living to fight another day assured the Counts of Poppi remained in possession of their territories in the Casentino for the next century and a half.

Often unfairly described by Florentine historians as shifty and craven, Guido Novello Guidi, Count of Poppi in the course of his long life he managed to keep the flag of Tuscan and Romagnol Ghibellinism flying even in the most adverse circumstances. Gifted with a nearly perfect sense of timing, Guidi knew when to strike and when to retreat, allowing him in a number of occasions to adroitly extricate himself from impending disasters, as he did at Campaldino. Giovanni Villani, *Nuovo cronica*, Chigiano L VIII 296, Vatican, Apostolic Library. (DEA Picture Library)

OPPOSING FORCES

It is important to recognize in the Guelphs and Ghibellines of 1289 two distinctly separate armies. Where other battles from the time might feature the same types of troops, armed and armoured in roughly the same way, and with similar training and experience, with Campaldino we see an example of the future of medieval warfare. Here the traditional medieval cavalry-dominated army was to face a force of non-traditional troops. The same would follow at Courtrai in 1302, at Bannockburn in 1314, at Mortgarten in 1318 and at Cassel in 1328.

It is also important to note that we have much better records for the Guelph army, both because of the richness of Florentine documentary and narrative sources – including the two most prominent chroniclers – and because the Arentine civic records were destroyed by fire, leaving only episcopal sources to draw from. Although, as the Ghibelline army was composed largely of lords and their retinues, we can compare them with similar contemporary forces.

THE GUELPH ARMY

From the extant sources we know the Guelph army of 1289 to have numbered around 12,000 combatants, necessitating a huge logistical effort. The Florentines, on whom fell most of the campaign's burden, had flexed their supply muscles to a shirt-splitting point. Each of the city's *sesti* elected a number of officials: in charge of 'mules and animals'; oversight of victualling operations; tasked with distributing arrows and crossbow-bolts; responsible for arms and armour; and probably the army's lodgings. These representatives commanded a large force of blacksmiths, carpenters, tailors, cooks, farriers, bakers and drivers, to which one should add camp followers such as sutlers, money changers and lenders, laundresses and, of course, prostitutes, all under the watchful eye of yet another elected officer. With such a large mass of people it would have been easy for the expedition to turn into a shambles, and therefore strict orders were issued to the army during the march and while in camp, threatening fines or more severe penalties 'at the *podestà's* discretion' for straggling and creating disturbances.

This may have been easier said than done in the case of the aristocrats who composed the bulk of the mounted forces – proud, haughty and often a law to themselves: 'If a friend or kinsman of theirs incurred a penalty, they

connived with the magistrates and officials to hide his guilt, so he might go unpunished', according to Compagni's, admittedly biased, opinion. Certainly, any official would have trodden lightly when dealing with a powerful man such as Corso Donati; or with the riotous and arrogant Filippo Adimari, known as *Argenti* for his habit of shoeing his horse with silver and described by Giovanni Boccaccio as 'tall, brawny and strong, more than any other proud, irascible and choleric' (appropriately, Dante would place him in Hell among the wrathful); or with the brothers Stoldo, Tegghia and Berto Frescobaldi, from a family rich enough to finance the building of the Santa Trinita bridge in Florence. People like these were the cream of the *cavallata* – the levy of the Commune of Florence's militia cavalry – their wealth sufficient to own a personal warhorse. Vieri de' Cerchi's horse was worth 120 gold florins, equivalent to four years' gross earnings for a normal worker.

Service in the Florentine militia was mandatory for all male citizens between the ages of 15 and 70, a theoretical pool of roughly 25,000–30,000 individuals, but probably half that amount in reality once invalids, clergymen and paupers were removed. Parish registers were used to compile militia lists: those selected were divided in groups of 50, in turn split into two units of 25 – the *venticinquina* being a standard subdivision for both infantry and cavalry. The various foot 'twenty-fifths', each including an elected leader, were supposed to serve in rotation under the banner of one of the 20 'Standards of the People' (*Gonfaloni del Popolo*), three for every *sesto*, except for the districts of Oltrarno and San Pier Scheraggio which had four. Cavalrymen came under the banner of the *sesto* to whom they belonged.

Mounted service was mandatory for all those above a certain income and warhorses were not supposed to cost less than 30 florins or more than 70; although, again, the rich and powerful, for whom owning and flaunting an expensive mount was yet another status-symbol, often ignored these rules and paid sometimes many more than 70 florins. On the other hand, for

The city of Florence

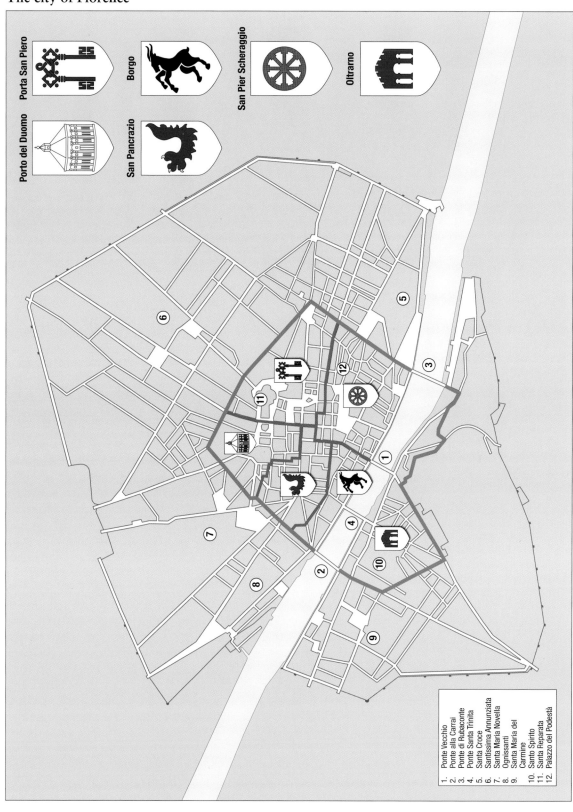

Porta San Piero

Borgo

San Pier Scheraggio

Oltrarno

Porto del Duomo

San Pancrazio

1. Ponte Vecchio
2. Ponte alla Carrai
3. Ponte di Rubaconte
4. Ponte Santa Trinita
5. Santa Croce
6. Santissima Annunziata
7. Santa Maria Novella
8. Ognissanti
9. Santa Maria del Carmine
10. Santo Spirito
11. Santa Reparata
12. Palazzo del Podestà

Florentine militia armed with pavises bearing the emblem of the Red Lion company, spears and, presumably, *mannaie aretine* (Aretine cleavers), intent on quelling a civic disturbance. This detail is from the so-called *Libro del Biadaiolo*. (Alamy)

some individuals even at the low end of the price scale, buying a warhorse could prove a serious financial burden and therefore various members of a lineage frequently owned *cavallata* mounts collectively. Dante probably fell into such a category, although the Alighieri as a family are known to have lived beyond their means in order to maintain their semi-spurious aristocratic status. Warhorses for the *cavallata* were registered in an official list and branded with the Commune's symbol, severe penalties being imposed on anyone who sold, swapped or used the mount thus selected for anything but military affairs. To prevent any fraudulent practice, the horses were described in detail, emphasizing their relevant physical traits: 'a bay, with a star on the forehead and with socks on the right legs', 'a sorrel, with fetlocks on the hind legs and skunked tailed'. Horse owners received between 40 and 50 florins a year for their upkeep, and on campaign a man-at-arms received between 10 and 15 *soldi* a day for the same purpose. Provisions existed for the compensation of any horse damaged or lost for military reason, although only once in the case of wounded mounts. All this imposed a considerable burden on the city's finances, necessitating extraordinary taxation to face the cost. This created a lot of resentment amongst the populace at large, resulting in repeated, albeit unsuccessful, attempts to saddle only the rich citizens with the expense, or not to pay militia cavalry for their service.

Those selected for the *cavallata* were supposed to serve in person, but could be substituted by kinsmen if impeded in any way; alternatively, they could hire mercenaries to take their place. Although *cavallata* duty was not always popular, in 1289 citizens constituted the bulk of Florence's mounted force, proudly displaying shield and banners emblazoned with their family arms.

Heraldry was already developed in Florence by the 1230s, and by the end of the century so well established that in the *Divine Comedy* Dante often refers to individuals or lineages simply by their coat-of-arms. The tinctures of Dante's own – party per pale, or and sable, a fess argent – followed a distinctly territorial pattern. Indeed, anyone looking at a fully equipped Florentine man-at-arms in 1289 would not only understand from his armorial bearings to which family he belonged, but also in which part of the city he lived. 'Or and sable' were common in the area around the church of San Martino al Vescovo, territorial connections with the once Imperial-controlled bishopric leading several kinships to adopt the tinctures of the Imperial arms: 'or, an eagle displayed sable'. Families of more recent origin, or lesser social standing, appear to have attached themselves heraldically to their more prestigious neighbours. The Giugni, once in the shadow of the Nerli, took on the latter's tinctures of 'or, gules and argent': 'pally argent and gules, a fess or' of the Nerli; 'gules, three bullocks hooves argent, a chief or' for the Giugni. Significantly, when the Nerli moved to the Oltrarno *sesto* in the first half of the 13th century, their new neighbours the Frescobaldi adopted arms similar to the Giugni's, substituting the hooves with chess-rooks.

It is unclear if in Florence certain heraldic partitions were connected with political factionalism. Several staunchly Guelph families, the Donati, the Buondelmonti and the Adimari adopted the 'party per fess' for their arms. However, drawing a general pattern is not entirely possible: the Ghibelline Caponsacchi and Abati sported a pale, but so did the Guelph Pepi and Pilli.

Armorial bearings were the same for all members of one family, marks of cadency being a later and personal addition. Crests, still in their infancy in 1289, were also a matter of individual choice and taste, unlike what appears to what was happening in the rest of Europe. Franco Sacchetti, writing in the late 14th century, records the amusing story of a Florentine gentleman being challenged to a duel by a German knight, both having the same crest of a demi-bear rampant; the matter ended with the business-minded Florentine selling his crest to the German and buying a different one with the profits.

Notwithstanding its flashiness, as a fighting force the Florentine cavalry had a reputation for ill discipline. The best of the city's mounted forces was lost with the exile or ostracism of the Ghibelline aristocrats, and the affluent *popolani* that took their place could hardly be considered of the same quality.

The impression of the seal of the Florentine Sozzo Guicciardini (*c*.1293) gives a very good idea of the appearance of the militia cavalry at the time of Campaldino. The small, fan-like crest on his great helm could be a sign of rank or simply an aesthetic affectation. (Gallerie degli Uffizi, Gabinetto Fotografico)

At Montaperti, in 1260, the Florentine horse had taken to its hooves when the going got tough, although a later narrative, dutifully reported by Villani, attributes this flight to the knowledge that treason was at work within their ranks. At Colle Val d'Elsa, nine years later, the Florentine cavalry launched a headlong assault on the Sienese-Imperialist mounted force despite being outnumbered two to one. Villani attributes the subsequent Guelph success to divine intervention, 'since the action was not considered either wise or well-thought from a military standpoint', and disaster only avoided by the careful planning and ability of the French commander Jean Britaud.

The men-at-arms provided to the Guelph League by Charles of Naples were, instead, among the finest in Europe, their standing established 75 years before at Bouvines and, more recently, at Benevento. Although the French reputation for invincibility had been dented at Forlì in 1282, their cavalry was nevertheless formidable and a welcome addition to the 600 or so members of the Florentine *cavallata*. Although often described as mercenaries since in Florentine pay, the French cavalry hardly fell in such a category as their wages were part of the political quid pro quo between the Guelph League and Charles of Naples. Florence and other Italian city-states did employ mercenary troops, but it is unclear if they were intended primarily for field or garrison duty. In 1289, Siena had in its service 80 horsemen under Bernardo da Rieti, who had been knighted the year before by the Florentines for his service against the Pisans. On the whole, Siena could never count on more than 300 militia cavalry and relied heavily on mercenary cavalry for its field armies. It is possible that the serious losses suffered by the Sienese at Pieve al Toppo the year before had forced them to field more mercenaries than usual, although many citizens are known to have served as cavalrymen in the 1289 campaign. Prominent among the latter for wealth and wit, the poet Cecco Angiolieri, later famous for his ribald rhymes, who may have met his Florentine counterpart, Dante, on this occasion.

Despite what most chronicles would have us believe, the other Guelph towns and lords in central Italy do not appear to have lived up to their stated commitments when it came to troops. Compagni tells us that Lucca and Pistoia each promised to send 200 horsemen, with contemporary documents

This illumination from the *Codex Manesse* was painted in Zurich *c.*1304–40. It depicts four infantry soldiers being pelted by stones while besieging a fortification. All wear mail armour, with two in mail coifs, one in a kettle hat without coif and the last in a conical helmet without coif. Two are aiming their crossbows at those atop the fortification, with one holding a pavise to protect him from stones and a torch perhaps to fire the mine which the first appears to be making using a hoe or axe. A fifth soldier, the bannerman, has been struck on the head by a stone and lies motionless on the ground. (Photo by DeAgostini/Getty Images)

confirming the strength of Lucca's contingent; however, according to Villani, the combined forces of the two cities amounted to about half that number, 150 and 60 respectively. On the other hand, the same author states that Volterra, with a population roughly the same as Pistoia, sent 40 knights to join the Guelph host. Probably Compagni is nearer to the mark in giving 1,300 total men-at-arms, compared to Villani's 1,600, although the latter has Narbonne's retinue as numbering 400 'soldiers in Florentine pay'. It is not impossible that Amauri's retinue included also a few hundred mounted sergeants, or light cavalrymen known as *berrovieri*, employed for scouting and raiding. Thus, Villani's total probably includes *all* mounted troops and Compagni's only the heavy cavalry.

The allied contingents included both horse and foot, the latter going to increase the already substantial Florentine infantry: the artisans, the small tradesmen and the workers who were not just the backbone of the *popolo*, but also of the city's economy. For this very reason, only a portion of Florence's militiamen, other than the cavalry, would be on campaign at any given time, at most the selected *venticinquine* of three *sesti* in the case of a major expedition. Attempting to raise a larger force would mean removing a substantial amount of the city's workforce, and therefore damaging its economy. In the case of a defeat, the social and material cost could be well nigh crippling. At Montaperti, the Florentine citizenship had sent into the field the infantry of five *sesti* and suffered 2,500 killed and 1,500 taken prisoner, the vast majority from the 'best households of the *popolo*', according to Villani. These losses represented about 12 per cent of the city's male population at the time, about double that percentage if the productive classes are

Illumination from the famous Luttrell Psalter (British Library Add. MS 42130), dated c.1320–1340, depicting a soldier placing the string of a crossbow onto a belt hook and, with his foot into the stirrup on the front of the bow, stepping down to load it. (British Library, London, UK / © British Library Board. All Rights Reserved / Bridgeman Images)

This fresco of Iberian infantry dates to the period of Campaldino. While it is difficult to determine what is worn under the soldiers' surcoats, or what material is used for the coifs each soldier wears (which mostly match the surcoats in colour), no distinctive mail armour is seen. This, plus the bare legs, spears and dagger-length swords suggests these are militia. The single helmeted soldier at the head of the force is certainly the leader. At Campaldino, most militia would have been better armed and armoured, having been equipped from their cities' arsenals. (Photo by Prisma/UIG/ Getty Images)

considered. Even if by 1289 the population of Florence had increased to over 80,000, it was still paramount to avoid as much as possible casualties at the Montaperti level. Therefore, even with three *sesti* on campaign, the Florentine city infantry probably did not exceed 3,000, including the '*marraiuoli et palaioli*' – literally 'hoers and polers', but probably used also to describe non-specialist infantry.

Florence, however, already had a sizeable territory outside its walls (*contado*), divided into military and administrative districts called *leghe* (leagues). In times of war, the *leghe* attached to the *sesti* taking the field were required to furnish a certain number of men to the main army; this levy was organized through country parishes. The size of this levy in 1289 is uncertain, but from surviving documents we can estimate something between 2,500 and 3,000 men, to which one should add about a few hundred sappers and miners, also recruited among the country folk. The quality of these troops must have varied, but in no way were they 'cavalry fodder' as some more recent authors would have us believe. Indeed, they were supposed to take an active part in battle, although probably in the rear ranks of the army, plus perform all those tasks necessary for a campaign's successful outcome: repairing roads, creating field fortifications and destroying enemy crops and buildings.

At the core of Florence's infantry were the specialists: crossbowmen, archers, spearmen and pavisiers. By 1289, a tactical synergy had developed between these troops, the pavisiers using their large shields to cover the other infantry. This suited very well the part-time nature of a citizens' army, which did not allow extensive infantry training in battlefield manoeuvres

Injustice, painted in 1306 by Giotto in the Scrovegni Chapel, Padua, shows this vice in the guise of an unjust lord. Below, his *masnadieri* engage in murder, rape and robbery against unfortunate travellers. (Photo by Antonio Quattrone/ Archivio Quattrone/Mondadori Portfolio via Getty Images)

and therefore the militiamen were taught how to perform basic defensive/reactive actions. Besides, the structure of the *venticinquina* could easily be adapted to the combination of pavisiers, spearmen, crossbowmen and archers: eight sections of three people, with one officer. The specialists probably made up about half of Florence's city infantry, and their military and social status was reflected by their daily pay: four *soldi*, against the three for the other infantry. Crossbows were issued by the Commune and a general tax was levied to pay for the weapons. All those who received wages for their military service were known as *soldati*, despite those that would have us believe the term being applied only to mercenaries.

Villani gives the total number of Guelph infantry as 10,000, while Compagni simply states that they were 'many'. We know that Maghinardo da Susinana came with 300 foot soldiers together with his 20 horsemen and that the other Guelph contingents included infantry as well as cavalry. Given that Florence provided 6,000–6,500 infantrymen, when the forces of Bologna, Siena, Lucca, Pistoia, Volterra, Colle, Valdelsa, San Miniato and of various allied lords are added, we can safely assume Villani's estimate as near the mark.

Two knights kneel at prayer in the Chapel Capece Minutolo in the Cathedral of Naples. Dating to around the time of Campaldino, their mail armour is like that worn by the cavalry on both sides of the conflict. Of particular note is the binding of the mail coif to the head, probably with padding below, in anticipation of a Great Helm. The enlarged epaulettes worn by both were especially popular among German knights, a possible indication of Ghibelline sympathies. (Photo by DeAgostini/Getty Images)

THE GHIBELLINE ARMY

Little is known of the Ghibelline forces during the 1289 campaign, but from the evidence available we can put together a tentative picture. Villani talks about the Aretine *masnade*, referring specifically to those of Count Guidi of Poppi. The term *masnada* originally indicated the collection of a fief's servile retainers, but by the end of the 13th century it had come to signify a lord's armed retinue or, more simply, a group of closely linked individuals. In the former meaning, the status of the *masnadieri* could be anything from serfs to something akin to salaried soldiers. While a *masnada* is usually intended as a bunch of unruly thugs – for example, one Florentine chronicle of the 14th century mentions the Medici as employing *masnadieri* to exact revenge on their enemies – this was hardly the case when it comes to Guidi's and Bishop

This *c.*1290 bas relief by Andrea di Jacopo d'Ognabene, from the silver altar in Pistoia's cathedral, depicts several soldiers with swords and bucklers, the two on the right also have mail collars, indicating mail hauberks worn underneath the clothes. These soldiers are arguably *masnadieri* of a local lord. (Photo by DeAgostini/ Getty Images)

Ubertini's retainers. Villani describes the Ghibelline host as composed of 'very fine men' (*molto bella gente*) and all 'practised in weapons and in war'. This same may not have been completely true for Arezzo's militia cavalry; these appear to have been a small number, the eviction of the Guelphs from the city and the humbling of the Aretine *popolo* having reduced the number of citizens willing to fight for Ubertini's regime. In any case, contrary to what had happened in Florence, in Arezzo the nobility had always held greater sway over communal political life, resulting in a much-weakened popular militia.

Such deficiencies were more than compensated for by the presence in the Imperialist army of many feudal lords with their retinues: 'the flower of the Ghibellines of Tuscany, of the Marches, of the Duchy [of Spoleto] and of Romagna', according to Villani. These noblemen could rely on the services of the 'good men' (*boni homines*), senior retainers often with substantial holdings of their own. In this way, someone like Count Guidi of Poppi could field a large cavalry force, stated to be around 150 men. The quality of their equipment is a matter of speculation. Many fiefs were in poor mountain areas, the various cities having encroached on the fertile plains since the beginning of the 12th century. In most cases feudal lords relied for their economic survival on selling timber, limited agricultural resources, tolls and customs, and, often, highway robbery under thin legal disguises

Another illumination from the *Codex Manesse* (Zurich, *c.*1304–40), it depicts a battle being fought close enough to a castle to be seen by enthralled female spectators. One army consists almost entirely of knights wearing great helms topped by very stylised headpieces (these, fashionable among Imperial knights, were usually attached to the top of the helmet for decoration but removed before engaging in combat or tournament; they would not have been worn at Campaldino). All are dressed in full mail armour. Their obviously poorer opponents have both cavalry and infantry. One horseman wears a great helm or bascinet with visor, while a second wears a kettle hat. They too are covered in mail, although their infantry appears to be wearing only cloth-covered coats of plates, conical helmets without face protection and carrying kite-shaped shields or pavises for protection. (Photo by Prisma/ UIG/Getty Images) (a member of the Malaspina family once answered the reprimands of Emperor Frederick I about his thieving activities, stating that it was the only way to survive, given the poverty of his lands). We can surmise, however, that a good portion of the troops belonging to Guidi, Montefeltro, Pazzi di Valdarno and Ubertini had benefitted from the rich booty taken the year before at Pieve al Toppo, the arms and armour of the 300 horsemen of those killed and captured by Siena on that occasion sufficient for the needs of more than one third of the cavalry fielded by the Ghibellines in the late spring of 1289.

Unlike the case of the Guelph city militias opposing them, the Ghibellines had honed their skills both on the training ground and in the field, a synergy thus developing between the infantry and the cavalry allowing the former to operate offensively with the horsemen, exploiting any gap in the enemy lines produced by the men-at-arms. From evidence found in contemporary sources, the Ghibelline infantry appears to have included men equipped with *coltella* – literally 'daggers', but also short swords, for close quarter engagements, used in combination with the buckler frequently seen

This Simone Martini painting shows two infantrymen wearing coats of plates over their mail hauberks in this fresco, dated to *c*.1314. These can be distinguished by the pairs of rivets running along the outside of the soldiers' tunics. These rivets would have attached iron plates to the tunic. Documentary evidence shows such coats to have been in widespread use among foot soldiers by the mid-1290s and therefore more than likely present at Campaldino. It is interesting also to note the rare depiction of a helmet hanging from one of the infantrymen's belts. (Photo by Art Media/Print Collector/Getty Images)

in the artworks of the time. From artistic sources, we can deduce that the Ghibelline foot shared many of the weapons of their Guelph counterparts: staff weapons, spears and the ubiquitous *mannaia aretina* ('Aretine cleaver'). The limited amount of city militiamen meant that the Ghibellines had also fewer crossbows, long spears and pavises than their adversaries; however, this mattered little, given the offensive tactics of the Ghibelline forces.

This sculpted head of a soldier at Framlingham Castle dates to the 13th century and shows how a coif of mail fitted onto a soldier's head to protect his face and chin. Atop this he would have placed a great helm or open-faced helmet. (Alamy)

ARMS AND ARMOUR

As they are frequently depicted in illustrations and funerary effigies, the arms and armour of those knights and noble cavalry on the battlefield in 1289 are easily determined. The most contemporary of these depictions is the bas-relief effigy on the sarcophagus of Guillaume de Durfort, the French knight who had been sent by King Charles II of Anjou to assist in leading the Guelph army, and was killed doing so. It shows a soldier dressed head to foot in mail armour. Durfort wears mail torso armour that descends below his waist. This mail coat had been the traditional cavalry armour since Charlemagne ruled Europe – when it was called a byrnie. However, while the Carolingian byrnie was one piece and only covered the shoulders and biceps, separate mail pieces cover the entire arms of Durfort, ending in mail mittens protecting the hands. Two mail leggings covered the lower limbs: one the thighs and upper legs, and another the lower legs and feet. These pieces were tied with laces or belts securely to the torso armour.

Durfort also wears extra protection on the shins, top of the feet, knees and thighs in the form of solid armour pieces. Relatively recent, it is uncertain if these were made of metal (steel or bronze), *cuir bouilli* (hardened rawhide) or leather. That they are ornately decorated has led some historians to assume the *cuir bouilli*. While metal greaves start making their appearance in the mid-13th century, leather ones appear in the frescoes depicting knights in combat in the Palazzo Comunale of San Gimignano (*c.*1292). This could be construed as a Mediterranean fashion, or simply evidence of experiments happening during a transitional period in the field of individual protection. In the same vein, while coats-of-plates existed at this time, it is unclear how many of them were in circulation. Indeed, the paucity of artistic evidence in this regard would lead to the conclusion that they were still somewhat uncommon, although a 1277 Florentine contract for a company of 'English' cavalry lists among their armour coats-of-plates 'to be worn over their mail', but these troops must have been exceptionally well armed, as their monthly pay of 18 florins indicates. Durfort's fleur-de-lys on his surcoat may have been rivets for one such coat, as suggested by some authors, but evidence is inconclusive.

A mail coif covers the back of Durfort's head, his neck and his throat. Other knights from the time would attach their coifs over their chins and even across their mouths, but Durfort's coif is tied under his very prominent chin. This may only be for artistic reasons – to show his complete face as few warriors would leave their vulnerable chins unprotected, as any blow there, while likely not fatal, would break a chin or jaw, disabling them.

The Great Helm, a large cylindrical and flat-topped helmet that fitted entirely around the head, with openings cut into its front only for sight and breathing, was popular at the end of the 13th century. It descended below the chin, and was secured quite firmly to the middle of the wearer's head by an extra quilted arming cap directly under the top. It is quite possible that Durfort wore a Great Helm at Campaldino rather than the conical short helmet that covers his head above the eyes but not the face below it, although this smaller helmet would mean better communication for a leader. At this date, the open-faced helm appears to have been popular among Italians and southern French – indeed, it figures prominently in the frescoes visible in the Rocca di Angera (*c*.1290), near Varese, and in those found in the Tour Ferrande à Pernes-les-fontaines, in Provence (*c*.1285).

As a final defence, Durfort carries a triangular shield. These shields had been common for more than a century, replacing the longer kite-shaped versions. They were made of wood, covered by leather, and, as can be

While this mail armour and coif from the collection of the Royal Armouries is dated to the 15th century, it shows the torso and arm coverings that would have been worn at Campaldino. It also shows the type of mail coif that soldiers in that battle would have worn and how it could be attached to a helmet to protect neck, throat, chin and lower face. (Royal Armouries)

This Great Helm in the collection of the Royal Armouries dates a century later than the battle of Campaldino but shows how protective helmets like these could be. It also demonstrates how heavy they were and how much they restricted sight, breathing and communication. (Trustees of the Royal Armouries)

Bascinets like this one in the Bardini Museum, Florence, were popular in Italy from the 13th century onwards. The iron gorget shown here was not likely worn at Campaldino, however. (Authors' Collection)

clearly seen in Durfort's effigy, painted with its bearer's coat of arms.

Durfort carries two weapons: a long and thick sword, tapering from its hilt to a point around three feet in length, which he wields in upraised arm; and a dagger, which is sheathed and attached to his sword belt at his waist. These were the most popular weapons of cavalry at this time, although a few are known to have favoured hammers, maces or axes over swords.

Much of the horse's fittings and equipment on Durfort's monument are obscured by its covering. This appears to be made of cloth, perhaps quilted fabric, the most common material used since the later 12th century. Called a caparison, by the time of Campaldino it would frequently be emblazoned with the rider's colours or arms. Why Durfort's horse does not wear his arms is unknown, although as effigies were often painted when it was carved, it could be that over time they have simply fallen off. It is also possible that, as everyone looking at the monument would know it was Durfort's, his arms were not added as identifiers. Mail horse armours appear in artistic sources from around the middle of the 13th century, but caparisons often obscure them, and we cannot tell with Durfort's memorial if this is the case. Durfort's caparison does obscure the horse's saddle, however, although the high pommel and cantle tightly fitting around his lower torso are clear. The reins are simple but effective: military riders needed their horses to follow commands quickly, without hesitation, and needed not be confused by elaborate equipment.

How stereotypical Durfort's arms and armour were for knights in general at the end of the 13th century is unclear. Illustrations suggest a number of choices for those who could afford them. The styles of helmets and armour differed, and there were probably several varieties worn at Campaldino. Fashion and comfort determined much – as it does today – as did braggadocio, how much armour one could give up for fashion and comfort before risking one's life.

Whether Durfort's effigy also exemplifies what the militia cavalries wore is unknown. No similar artistic or literary depictions exist from Florence, or from anywhere else, at the end of the 13th or beginning of

the 14th century. This has led some arms and armour historians to believe that urban arsenals did not hold, nor militias wear or carry, anything near as expensive as the knight. Nor did the militia infantry wear what a lord could buy his infantry retinues. Such may be true for 1289; however, later evidence suggests it is not. Arsenal inventories of the 14th and 15th centuries prove the opposite, that those who served for a city or town, especially as rich as Florence or other Guelph towns sending troops to Campaldino, had the means to provide their militias with the best arms and armour available. This is further confirmed by depictions cast on the St James silver altarpiece in the cathedral of Pistoia before 1290, carved on the Oxford Chest of Flemish urban militias that fought at the battle of Courtrai in 1302 and painted on a Ghent wall of that city's militia who fought in the early Hundred Years War (the latter unfortunately now lost but recorded in modern drawings). All militiamen marching to and fighting in battles wear body-covering mail and mail coifs, with clear depictions (at least in the paintings) of plates covering the elbows and arms – likely also on the legs, although these are more difficult to see. Finally, the armour of soldiers found in mass graves buried after their defeat at the battle of Visby in 1361 show that even rural peasants – who are known to rest in these graves – wore cloth-covered coats of plates, not unlike those required to be worn in late 13th-century Florentine documents. Whether we can assume from these contemporary and later medieval sources that the militia and retinue infantries who fought at Campaldino wore the same armour is, and will likely remain, uncertain. However, we must also remember that Florence was filled with artisans and merchants who made and sold the most up-to-date armour in Europe, as evidenced in the 1296 order by Charles II that Florentine merchants provide him with 4,000 coats of plates – that number suggesting these were for the infantry. Florence and the other Guelph cities were wealthy, with a desire to display it. The militias were paid well while in service; they would also be outfitted well, both the cavalry and the infantry.

The infantry at Campaldino carried weapons like the cavalry, with two important exceptions. The first was the staff weapon, or pole arm, long-handled weapons with an axe-head, blade or hammer at the end. The earliest mention of a staff-weapon is in a Catalan document of AD 977 which refers to a *guisarme*, described as a long-hafted weapon with an extremely long, axe-shaped head; several artistic depictions follow over the next three centuries. By the end of the 13th century footsoldiers were using several different types of staff weapons – the names halberd, glaive, bill, partizan, morgenstern (or morning star), holy water sprinkler, goupillon,

Swords like this from the late 13th/early 14th centuries were used on the battlefield of Campaldino by all soldiers. The weight of the pommel and cross-hilt balanced the blade, although the shape and length of similarly dated swords differed sufficiently enough to suggest personal preference was a major factor. (Trustees of the Royal Armouries)

pollaxe and *mannaia aretina* (Aretine cleavers) all appear before the end of the Middle Ages – and it is not clear which type was favoured by the infantry at Campaldino. Certainly, the silver altarpiece in Pistoia depicts staff weapons carried by several of the soldiers; some of these are prime candidates for the Aretine cleavers that are so frequently mentioned in documents of the period.

The second distinct infantry weapon was the crossbow. A much more complex and technologically sophisticated weapon – a short, heavy bow stave attached to a stock fitted with release mechanism (usually a nut of horn or ivory) to which the string could be pulled, a bolt laid within and launched by pulling on a trigger (a lever attached to the release) – the crossbow became popular in Europe in the two centuries preceding the battle of Campaldino. They were impressive weapons, with Anna Comnena, an 11th-century Byzantine princess, describing them as able to 'transfix a shield, cut through a heavy iron breastplate and resume their flight on the far side.... Such is the crossbow, a truly diabolical machine. The unfortunate man who is struck by it dies without feeling the blow; however strong the impact he knows nothing of it'. This power led a pope, Urban II, in 1096–97 and the Second Lateran Council in 1139 to condemn its use among Christians, although these prohibitions seem only to have pushed up the wages of those soldiers skilled in shooting them. Most crossbows at Campaldino would have been spanned by the archer placing his foot into a stirrup at the end of the bow with the bowstring on a hook secured to his belt, a process that took sufficient time to indicate that a crossbow was shot only a few times during a pitched battle.

To protect crossbowmen while loading, a large shield, the *pavise*, was invented – likely in Pavia earlier in the 13th century, hence its name. Pavises could be carried by attendants (*pavesari*) or set up with a brace similar to

This 'quillon dagger' is from the collection of the Royal Armouries. Although it is English and dated 1371–99, it is almost identical to those found in 13th-century illustrations. (Trustees of the Royal Armouries)

This cloth-covered coat-of-plates, from Chalcis and today housed in the Metropolitan Museum of Art, is dated to *c*.1400, the earliest non-archaeological type of this armour to survive. Despite being a century later, illustrations from the time of Campaldino show that similar coats-of-plates would have been worn by men-at-arms in the battle. (Bashford Dean Memorial Collection, Bequest of Bashford Dean, 1928)

an easel. Infantry at Campaldino, especially those in the lords' retinue who were better trained, most likely made use of bucklers: small, often concave shields, held by a handle across the inside that was anchored by a hollow metal boss on the outside. These could be used by nimble soldiers to ward off blows and arrows while they wielded spears, swords and daggers against opponents and their horses.

Infantry helmets varied widely at the end of the 13th century. Rarely are infantry portrayed wearing Great Helms or other visored helmets in artistic representations. Most often they wear conical helmets covering either the top of the head above the ear, like that depicted on the Durfort effigy, or bascinets, conical or globular helmets which extended down to the base of the neck and forward to cover the rear of the cheeks. The so-called kettle hat, consisting of a close-fitting bowl with a wide, flat brim, was also popular for infantries of the time. Central Italian artworks show that the brim on helmets worn there were narrower than elsewhere in Europe, although the reason for this cannot be determined.

There were a large variety of staff weapons used by infantry troops during the Middle Ages. Rarely is a uniformity in these seen in depictions of medieval soldiers. The size and shape of the blade, whether there was a hook or point at the end, seemed to rely on an individual's soldiers' preference, as depicted in this Holkham Bible Picture Book illumination from the British Library (Additional 47682, f.14v), c.1327–35. Here the three infantry soldiers carry three entirely different staff weapons. (British Library)

These soldiers watching over the burning of a heretic wear mail armour and conical helmets yet are especially distinguished by their carrying bucklers for added protection. Bucklers were light and manoeuvrable shields, easily wielded by inexperienced soldiers, especially against blows from mounted opponents. They were favoured by those lightly equipped professionals who made up the Ghibelline *masnade*. (Heretics thrown into the fire, illumination from *Commentaire des coutumes de Toulouse*, 1296/ Tallandier /Bridgeman Images)

OPPOSING PLANS

During the Campaldino campaign, both the Guelphs and Ghibellines pursued long-term strategic goals. The main problem that we face today in understanding them is one of historical perspective: it is difficult for us to understand what by modern standards is nothing less than a lengthy, sluggish form of warfare, made essentially of raids and sieges, and in which political considerations apparently trumped effectiveness in the field. The men of the 13th century understood the limitations – logistic, economic, physical, and political – imposed on warfare. Therefore, the main objective of any campaign was the interdiction of enemy movements, while at the same time putting political pressure on the rival state (including, in Italy, running horse races under the walls of a besieged city) to make it lose credibility and force a regime change. Change could be desired for better political and economic ties, and for the guarantee of future alliances in wars. Raids could terrify rivals into submission; sieges could take their castles, towns and resources as pawns in negotiations. Battles were considered risky, to be avoided unless absolutely necessary.

A view of the battlefield from the rear line of Guelph troops, made up mostly of militia infantries from Florence and allied cities. A soldier standing in this line could see Poppi Castle in the distance; however, how many and what kind of troops opposed him would have been largely obscured by his own lines stretched across the field in front of him. (Authors' Collection)

THE GUELPH PLAN

Although ostensibly a Florentine-led enterprise, in 1289 the objectives of the campaign against Arezzo were mutual for all the members of the Guelph coalition. From Arezzo departed a number of roads, heading towards the Tiber Valley and the Marches, and towards Romagna, linking up with the crucially important salt route in the Po Valley. To the south and east, Aretine territory overlapped the Via Francigena, which ran all the way to Rome and was a vital commercial artery for Siena. Ghibelline lords in the mountains north of Arezzo and in the upper Arno Valley

formed a chain of fortified settlements (*castella*), acting as a buffer for the Aretine Commune and connected with other fiefs across the Apennines through the so-called 'Monastery Road' that owed its name to the number of religious foundations found along the route. Not all the lords of the area were committed Ghibellines, for example the Guidi of Battifolle and of Romena sided with the Guelphs; yet, the Florentines tended to mistrust their feudal confederates, suspicious about where their ultimate allegiances really lay. The same was true for monastic congregations: in 1258 the Florentines executed Tesauro de' Beccheria, the abbot of Vallombrosa, believing he had been plotting with the then exiled Ghibellines to trigger a regime change in Florence.

Once Pisa went over to the Ghibellines in 1288, the Guelph League was confronted with the nightmarish situation of the Pisans joining forces with the Aretines, executing a flanking movement through the mountains after making inroads in the lower Arno Valley. This would sever the routes from Florence to Bologna. This nightmare became real with the arrival in Pisa of the first-class strategist, Guido di Montefeltro. Therefore, the Guelphs' decision to attack Arezzo via the Casentino had a quadruple objective: stopping any wavering lords from switching sides; confirming the loyalty of those allied to Florence; killing the chance of Pisans and Aretines from joining forces through control of the mountain routes; and putting political pressure on the enemy city. While the Guelph army was perfectly equipped for a field encounter, its main focus was on siege warfare and raiding – the best means to hamper the enemy's movements and lay bare the impotence of the Aretine regime to protect its people. This meant a deep penetration into Ghibelline territory, capturing strongholds that, if not demolished, could be used as logistic springboards to further the advance, or eventually used as bargaining chips for future peace negotiations.

The Guelph leaders, Amauri de Narbonne and Guillaume de Durfort, may have used this rising slope to anchor the rear units of their troops. As at other battles, they may have positioned the camp's carts on top to protect their supplies and contain their troops. (Authors' Collection)

A view of the battlefield from outside the front of the church of Certomondo. This is the likely position of the Ghibelline paladins and second cavalry line at the beginning of the battle as it gave their rearguard, commanded by Count Guido Novello Guidi and hidden in the unfinished cloister behind the church, the ability to enter the battle when tactically advantageous. (Authors' Collection)

Prepared as the army may have been for battle, the Guelph commanders were not keen to face the Ghibellines in the field. The risks involved were many and in case of defeat had potentially disastrous consequences, both politically and economically. It remained to be seen if the Ghibellines were prepared to dance to the Guelph tune.

THE GHIBELLINE PLAN

Faced with a mighty army descending upon them, the Ghibellines had the option either to engage it in battle or wear it down by forcing the Guelphs to be mired in one siege after another. However, such a strategy had a number of shortcomings. It would subject the Aretine countryside to untold ravishes for several months, and while counter-raiding could hope to draw away some Guelph forces to protect Florentine territory, at the same time detaching a considerable number of troops for such forays would inevitably weaken the Ghibellines' defensive capacity near home. From a political standpoint, the torching of the Aretine *contado* affected less the Commune of Arezzo itself than those lords whose lands formed a belt around the city. Therefore, some important Ghibelline leaders – Bishop Ubertini, Guglielmo de' Pazzi di Valdarno, Guido Novello Guidi and others – were faced with the prospect of having to invest considerable resources in protecting their territories. Bishop Ubertini's alleged willingness to come to terms with the Florentines by ceding the castles belonging to his diocese would also be a way to goad the Aretines in saddling themselves with the burden of their defence.

All this considered, one can well understand the Aretine leadership's vested interest in wanting the Guelph threat removed as soon as possible, and this could only be accomplished by a confrontation in the field – with the lingering hope that the enemy be cowered and forced to retreat by a simple show of force. Should battle be joined, the Ghibellines confided in their greater training and experience, being in this respect more than a match for their Guelph opponents that they 'held in contempt', according to Giovanni Villani. Should they be forced from the field, the Ghibellines always had the advantage of operating in a friendly territory, with the possibility of regrouping in one or more of their many strongholds in the area. So, as opposed to the Guelphs, a set-piece battle was an attractive option for the Ghibellines.

The Ghibellines were right in believing their opponents inferior. Unfortunately, as it turned out, all too right.

THE CAMPAIGN

RAID, SEIZE AND HOLD

Military operations started early in 1289, at the beginning of March, with the Ghibellines executing several raids into enemy territory. The Sienese were the first to feel 'the hard hand of war', the fortified towns of Isola and Buonconvento were fed to the flames by Count Guido Novello Guidi of Poppi in his capacity of *podestà* of Arezzo. The rest of the Sienese countryside was similarly ravaged, encouraging the Ghibelline lords under Siena's suzerainty to reaffirm once more their loyalty to the emperor. Florence was Guidi's next target, with a force of 400 cavalry and 3,000 infantry pillaging the Florentine upper Arno Valley. Rebuffed at the Florentine-held Incisa by the spirited resistance of the castle's defenders, the Ghibellines pushed on to San Donato in Collina, 12km from Florence, reducing it to ashes, together with the great elm tree planted in front of the local church. The Florentines could clearly see the hill of San Donato engulfed in smoke, and the government came under increasing pressure to act to stem the Ghibelline tide. Guidi's activities were as much a political threat as a military one, since Ghibelline successes in the field could easily sway undecided states to join the Imperialists – Percivalle Fieschi's continuing presence in Arezzo did not bode well in that sense. In mid-March, the arrival in Pisa of Guido di Montefeltro increased such a peril, as Montefeltro quickly reorganized the Pisan militia into a credible fighting force and started launching raids against Guelph territories, taking several fortified places and threatening the communication routes in the lower Arno Valley. Should the still unaligned lords in northern Tuscany side in force with the Imperialists, their lands, fortifications and roads would form a strong territorial chain across the length of the Apennine Mountains. This would allow the Pisans to link up with the main Ghibelline force in the region.

Dominating the *Casentino* countryside, the Guidi castle of Poppi was constructed in the years prior to the battle of Campaldino. It is to here that Guido di Guidi retreated during the battle. (Authors' Collection)

The Campaldino Campaign

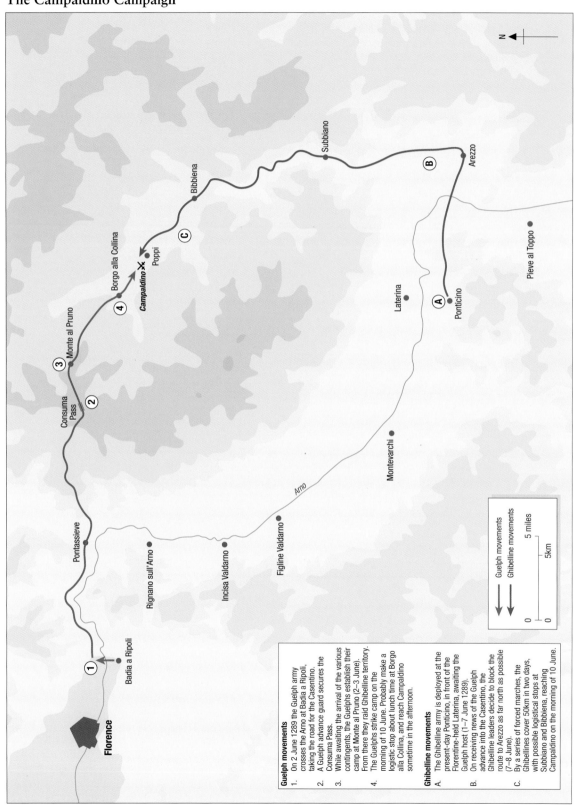

Guelph movements

1. On 2 June 1289 the Guelph army crosses the Arno at Badia a Ripoli, taking the road for the Casentino.
2. A Guelph advance guard secures the Consuma Pass.
3. While awaiting the arrival of the various contingents, the Guelphs establish their camp at Monte al Pruno (2–3 June). From there they raid Ghibelline territory.
4. The Guelphs strike camp on the morning of 10 June. Probably make a logistic stop about lunch time at Borgo alla Collina, and reach Campaldino sometime in the afternoon.

Ghibelline movements

A. The Ghibelline army is deployed at the present-day Ponticino, in front of the Florentine-held Laterina, awaiting the Guelph host (1–7 June 1289).
B. On receiving news of the Guelph advance into the Casentino, the Ghibelline leaders decide to block the route to Arezzo as far north as possible (7–8 June).
C. By a series of forced marches, the Ghibellines cover 50km in two days, with possible logistical stops at Subbiano and Bibbiena, reaching Campaldino on the morning of 10 June.

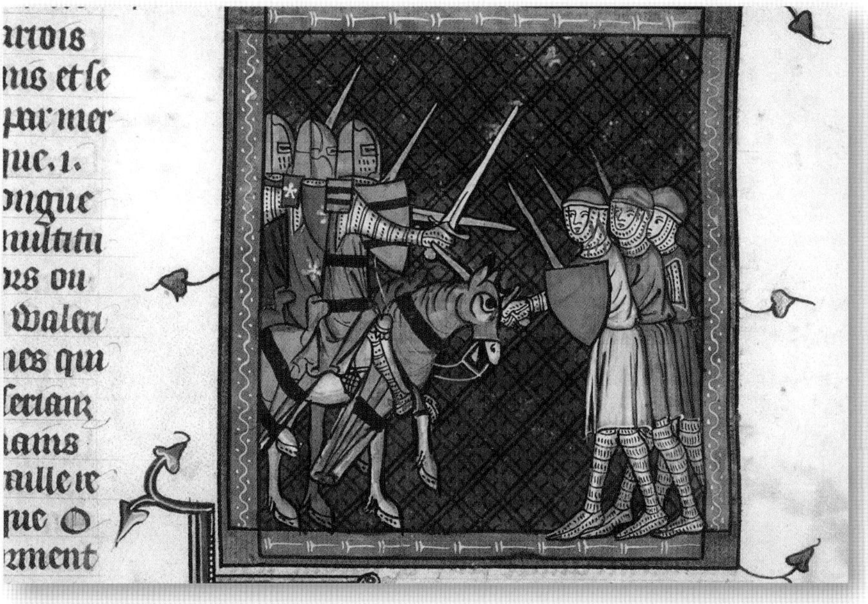

This scene from an early 14th-century French manuscript (British Library, Royal 16 G VI, f. 381), shows medieval cavalry and infantry as many would have appeared on the battle of Campaldino. The cavalry wear Great Helms, carry triangular shields and are clad completely in mail armour from head to foot, with metal plates covering that mail on the knees and shins. Their heraldry is shown on their shields, surcoats, epaulettes and their horses' caparisons. The infantry opposing them wear mail armour (with no plate reinforcement), carry slightly smaller shields and wear conical helmets. Although, their surcoats and shields are bare of heraldry, at Campaldino these soldiers would have carried the arms of their lords or, for the urban militias from Florence and elsewhere of their families or *masnade*. (British Library)

To counter such a possibility, the Florentines launched their own raids into Aretine territory in April, while trying to bring their allies together for a major expedition against the enemy city. In the same month, a gathering in Empoli of the representatives of Guelph cities voted for 'total war' against Arezzo. This, however, created a problem of leadership, as the death of Ranuccio Farnese at Pieve al Toppo had deprived the Guelph League of its commander-in-chief. Finding a suitable replacement would take time, Siena, Lucca or even smaller states loath to be led by a Florentine – local pride combined with the belief that no one in Florence had the necessary experience or ability to lead the coalition made such an idea totally impractical. A number of Romagnol lords did possess the necessary military qualities, but their loyalties were often suspect. One such lord was Maghinardo Pagani da Susinana, considered the acme of fidelity by the chronicler, Giovanni Villani, but Dante would acidly comment that Susinara had a habit of changing factions 'from summer to winter'. In reality, it would appear that Maghinardo's own political interests often caused him to side both with the Ghibellines in the Romagne and with their opponents in Tuscany. The Guelph league tried to solve the problem by hiring the Roman baron Baldovino da Supino with his retinue of 400 cavalry. 'But the pope retained him, and so he did not come', wrote the chronicler Dino Compagni, the Florentines suspecting the pontiff's alleged Ghibelline sympathies as the reason.

Luckily, at the beginning of May the recently liberated King Charles II of Naples arrived in Florence on his way to be crowned by the pope in Rieti. The Florentines had received intelligence that the Ghibellines intended to ambush the king's small retinue en route; therefore, the city willingly provided Charles with an escort of 800 cavalry and 4,000 infantry, many of the latter drawn from the *villanata*, the country levy drawn from the various Florentine *leghe*. In return, the king agreed to designate a leader for the Guelph alliance, picked from his followers. The choice fell on Amauri of Narbonne, dubbed a knight for the occasion. The bestowed knighthood was supposed to give Amauri greater authority, but, given Narbonne's youth and inexperience, real leadership rested in the hands of his deputy, Guillaume de Durfort. Charles also agreed to leave behind 100 French knights as a boost for the Guelph forces.

The rural population was powerless in the face of the endemic warfare that frequently took their lives and destroyed their livelihoods, as underscored by this depiction of the killing of Job's servants by Taddeo Gaddi, which was painted in the 1340s. The savagery of the killings in the foreground is compounded by the herd being driven away in the background. (Photo by Miguel Hermoso Cuesta/CC BY-SA 4.0)

As soon as the king departed, Florence decided to settle the score with Arezzo. Not everyone in the city backed the new campaign; the *popolani*, in particular, considered the war unjust, besides having a strong dislike for the magnates, the main supporters of the military option, whom they accused of desiring war for the sake of their own aggrandizement. However, the magnates had their way, and on 13 May the Florentine army received its war banners in the course of a solemn ceremony in the presence of the city's most important political and social bodies: the priors of the guilds, the knights, the clergy and the *podestà*. It was the *podestà* to whom, in theory, fell the task of leading the army in the field. The standards were blessed and prayers offered to God and the saints, especially St John the Baptist. From the cathedral, the insignia were carried in procession to the expedition's starting point, on this particular occasion to the Badia a Ripoli, from where the road led to Arezzo through the upper Arno Valley. The banners were protected day and night by a strong military contingent, selected in rotation from the city's *sesti* and parishes.

The preparations for the campaign picked up speed. Messengers were sent across the length of Florence's territory, bells rung and beacons lit, ordering the communities in the countryside to send men, transports and victuals to the city or be ready to join the army on route. 2000 *lire* worth of supplies were allotted to Montevarchi, the logistic springboard for the forthcoming expedition. Allied contingents would take some time to arrive; meanwhile, the Florentine government distributed arms and equipment to its militia, raised money by imposing a five percent tax on income, hired professional soldiers for garrison and field duty, and set about quashing any potential form of internal threat. Many Ghibellines still lived in Florence, readmitted into the city after the peace brokered by Cardinal Latino Orsini in 1280; now, they came again under suspicion, and in order to nip any sort of disloyal action in the bud, dozens of them were sent once more into exile, although within the boundaries of Florence's territory.

Sometime after 13 May, a meeting was held in Florence's Baptistery to hammer out a strategy for the impending campaign. The main point discussed was which route to take to enter Aretine country. Many upheld the former decision to march through the Valdarno, since this would stop any Ghibelline raids into Florence's lands. However, a number of those present pointed instead to the Casentino as their favoured direction of advance, arguing that otherwise the Guelph forces risked being drawn deep into enemy territory and eventually becoming entrapped – the painful lesson of Pieve al Toppo still loomed large. The Casentino option was also backed by the Aretine exiles, some of them with castles in the area, fearing that if left unprotected they might lose them to the Ghibellines; besides, a Guelph force in the Casentino would assure that those lords playing a waiting game would not go over to the other side and the Ghibelline ones, such as Count Guido Novello Guidi of Poppi, would be more interested in defending their fiefs rather than raiding. A secret ballot returned a majority favouring the northern route to Arezzo, and so, despite a lot of grumbling and misgivings, the war standards were moved from the Badia a Ripoli to the other side of the Arno River, probably in front of the church of San Pietro a Varlungo, on the road to the Casentino.

Another factor played a part in the Guelphs' decision. As befitted his reputation as a consummate survivor, the Bishop of Arezzo, Guglielmino degli Ubertini, sometime before had secretly sought an agreement with the Florentines to preserve his own power and avoid the devastation of the bishopric's possessions by hostile troops. As a result, he proposed to cede Bibbiena and other diocesan strongholds by becoming Florence's vassal, in exchange for an annual pension of 3,000 florins guaranteed by the Cerchi bank. The offer was tempting, but the members of the Florentine bi-monthly government of April–June 1289 were divided as to whether to accept it or not. The *popolani* were unwilling to become embroiled in another war with Arezzo, a war they felt was inevitable should this deal go through. In the end, the chronicler Dino Compagni, one of the priors for that bimestre – and certainly one of the reasons his chronicle is so full of information for this period – was given the task of exploring the matter further, and he in turn entrusted Durazzo Vecchietti, recently knighted by Ubertini, to act as a go between.

The bishop, however, was playing a double game – Villani acidly comments that 'at one time he intended to betray the Florentines and his own Aretines' – having no intention to cede Bibbiena or any other episcopal fortress, but rather saddle his fellow citizens with their defence. He tried to convince them to reinforce Bibbiena and come to terms with the Florentines, or he would do so instead. This so enraged the Ghibellines, that Ubertini only avoided being lynched thanks to the intervention of his nephew, Guglielmo de' Pazzi di Valdarno, who stated bluntly that he did not want to be an accessory in the murder of a kinsman. In reality, the Aretines had been hoping for a Guelph inroad into the Casentino, counting on their enemies getting tied down and tired by the prolonged sieges of strongholds not directly belonging to the city and thus deflecting most of the ravaging away from Arezzo's territories. Naturally, Ubertini and the count of Poppi had no intention of looking on passively while the invaders torched their lands, and the bishop had simply tried, in his own devious way, to forestall any material losses for himself and his diocese.

Negotiations having come to nothing, on 2 June the Guelph army moved out of Florence at the sound of the war-bell known as the *martinella*. We do not know the exact order of the march, except that the French under

Narbonne held the rear of the column. However, the breakdown of the Florentine army on the move can be gleaned from the so-called *Libro di Montaperti* from 1260 (although in general one should be cautious in applying it to the Campaldino campaign). In August 1260, the Florentines marched into Sienese territory with the archers and crossbowmen in front, followed by the cavalry and the infantry of three *sesti*, then by the baggage, the remaining *sesti*, and the allied contingents bringing up the rear. The Florentine government was clearly very worried about taking 'bad roads' into the mountains, fearful that if the expeditionary force came under attack, the outcome would have been disastrous; luckily for the Guelphs 'God did not allow this', to use Compagni's words, despite the inevitable slowness of the march along the winding road up steep hills. In June 1289, there was a need to act quickly before the Ghibellines, deployed so as to block the Valdarno road, got wind of what was happening. This probably meant sending forward a strong mobile contingent to secure the Consuma Pass leading into the Casentino – indeed, Villani implies as much. Besides, not all the allied forces had yet arrived, and so the Florentines needed a strong position in which to pitch camp while building the Guelph army up to strength.

The selected spot was Monte al Pruno, a barren hill from where it is possible to overlook the entire Casentino: there was also a freshwater spring nearby, with the added advantage of being near the small monastery of Santa Maria a Pietrafitta, to provide logistical and spiritual support. Once a suitable force was assembled at Monte al Pruno and the location secured, the Guelphs launched a series of raids in the area – Dante calls them the *gualdane* – looting, burning and taking prisoners among the country folk. As most of the damage inflicted was on the count of Poppi's lands, it forced the Ghibellines to retreat from the vulnerable Florentine frontier in the Valdarno.

THE ROAD TO CAMPALDINO

The metal *marzocco* – the lion rampant or sejant, symbol of the city of Florence – was placed on top of the Guelph headquarters' pavilion at Monte

An army on the march. Trumpeters precede the cavalry in the vanguard, followed by drummers giving tempo to the infantry. (Victory of the Sienese troops over the English mercenaries at Val di Chiana in 1363, c.1364 (fresco), Vanni, Lippo (fl.1344–76)/ Palazzo Pubblico, Siena, Italy/ De Agostini Picture Library/ Bridgeman Images)

al Pruno and could be seen from miles away. Resplendent in the June light, it was a harbinger of doom for the entire Casentino, as the Florentines and their allies laid waste the count of Poppi and Bishop Ubertini's lands. The Ghibellines had been expecting an enemy invasion from the Valdarno and deployed their forces near the Florentine-held Laterina in order to block any inroads into Aretine territory from the west and the south-west. Before long, probably around 7 or 8 June, they learned of the Guelph whereabouts, as fleeing peasants flooded into Arezzo and other towns quickly spreading tales of arson and destruction. Realizing they had been outsmarted, the Ghibellines marched north in all haste, Count Guidi and Bishop Ubertini having an extra reason for speed, since their lands had been the target of Guelph raids and they feared for the strategically important fortresses of Poppi and Bibbiena. It is a tribute to the organizational skill of the Ghibellines that their army managed to cover in about two days the roughly 50km from Laterina to Poppi up steep mountain roads, with carts in their wake and without the whole operation turning into chaos. The Ghibelline leaders likely reckoned that it would take time for their enemies to complete the build up of their forces at Monte al Pruno before descending into the valley below.

The Ghibellines bested the Guelphs, arriving in the early afternoon of 10 June at Poppi and deploying their army in front of the castle on a plain known as Campaldino. They had stolen a march on the enemy and blocked the road to Arezzo. Moreover, they had chosen a very good defensive position, with the river Arno on their left and rising ground on their right, on which stood the Franciscan convent of Certomondo. From Poppi for about two-thirds of a mile, the field of Campaldino is less than 450m in width, compressed as it is by the elevated road and the steep banks of the Arno. The Ghibelline position also had the advantage of having at its back Count Guidi's castle, a refuge if need be, and the road leading to the monastery of Camaldoli and over the Appenines – a vital route for retreating or receiving reinforcements from

Monte al Pruno on the road to Poppi. The barren wide swathe of land gives a good idea of the dimensions of the Guelph camp, stretching all the way up to the peak and commanding an ample view of the Casentino. The reflection of the sun on the metal *Marzocco* atop Narbonne's tent would have been clearly visible from the valley below, a herald of disaster for the country folk unfortunate enough to be in the path of a Guelph raiding party. (Authors' Collection)

the Romagna. To reach this, one had to cross a ford at the junction between the Arno and the Sova stream, easy to pass even for a substantial force in the dry season.

A topographical riddle is attached to these water bodies. In the *Divine Comedy*, Dante does not mention the Sova but talks of the Archiano River meeting the Arno 'at the foot of the Casentino', and from the context he is clearly indicating that this happens near Poppi. The Archiano does flow into the Arno, but nearly 11km downstream in the proximity of Bibbiena (which the poet, incidentally, does not consider part of the Casentino). Since Dante could not have made such a blatant mistake – he knew the area not just because of the 1289 campaign, but also because of the 1289 campaign, but also from spending time there during his subsequent exile from Florence – it has been argued, with little evidence, that at the time the Archiano's course was different and running nearer to Poppi than today. Others maintain instead that the Sova at the time was more simply the western branch of the Archiano, yet Dante mentions the latter as born above 'the hermitage' of Camaldoli, while in reality its origins are nearly 16km to the east, at the Passo dei Mandrioli. The Sova, on the other hand, begins to flow at Poggio Muschioso, between the monastery and the hermitage of Camaldoli, some of its tributaries originating even higher up in the mountains. It could well be that the term 'Archiano' covered all the water bodies flowing down from that part of the Appenines, or, more simply, that Dante found the term better than Sova for poetic reasons.

Once at Campaldino, the Ghibellines begin to prepare the field for what appeared to be an inevitable encounter. Irrigation ditches, that still today

The Arno Valley, as seen from the road from Monte al Pruno to Poppi, visible in the background through the summer haze. The advancing Guelphs beheld a similar view on the afternoon of 10 June, still oblivious of the awaiting Ghibelline army deployed just a few miles away. (Authors' Collection)

48

A military camp from the time in a detail of a fresco by Simone Martini in the Palazzo Pubblico of Siena, *c.*1330. The large pavilions depicted were for senior officers: less important or affluent individuals got huts comprising a simple wooden frame covered with straw, sometimes sitting on an underlying bed of dried mud. Note the wooden stockade in the foreground. (Photo by: Universal History Archive/UIG via Getty Images)

crisscross the plain, were filled and the ground levelled so as not to impede cavalry and infantry manoeuvres. The real strength of the enemy was still unknown, nevertheless the Ghibellines predicted correctly that they would have to fight – unless the Guelphs opted for a perilous and humiliating retreat. But should battle be joined, then the Guelphs would be funnelled on a ground chosen by their adversaries, thus negating their numerical advantage. The preparations for battle were done in the nick of time, for the enemy host could already be seen descending the Casentino road.

The Guelphs probably struck camp in the morning of 10 June, slowly making their way towards Poppi. Although the distance is about 16km, the numerous carts must have slowed down the march considerably, to which one should add the necessary stops for resting and eating. According to some sources the invading army halted a while at Borgo alla Collina, a castle 5km from Campaldino owned by Guido Guidi of Battifolle, a cousin of the count of Poppi but staunchly pro-Florentine in his allegiance. It is possible that part of the army took the longer route, south of Monte al Pruno, that unites with the main one at Borgo alla Collina; but this would have meant an even longer delay. Therefore, the Guelph vanguard must have reached Campaldino sometime in the afternoon, after more than eight hours on the move, to behold the Ghibelline army already in place. This came somewhat as a surprise and Amauri de Narbonne, informed of the fact, rode over to reconnoitre the situation. What he likely saw was a reduced enemy force, part of the Ghibelline horse and foot not visible due to an already enacted battle plan. Unable to believe his eyes, not least because of a certain amount of youthful arrogance, Narbonne is reported to have exclaimed: 'Either we have been tricked, or these men are insane!' He had good reasons to suspect a trap, undoubtedly aware that so many battles had been won by subterfuge rather than valour. Moreover, the idea that treachery had been the reason for the Florentine defeat at Montaperti was already an integral part of Guelph lore.

Narbonne was not the only one with misgivings. Buonconte di Montefeltro climbed up the tower of Poppi to make a better assessment of the enemy forces. What he saw was sufficiently disquieting to suggest to Bishop Ubertini that fighting should be avoided, knowing by experience that, to use the words of the early 15th-century Florentine statesman, Gino Capponi, 'before a battle has ended no one can be certain of victory, no matter the

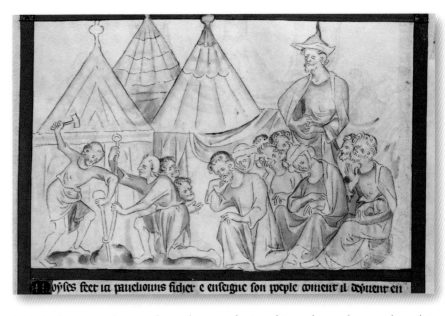

The camp of a huge army could stretch over hectares. As shown in this illumination from the Queen Mary's Psalter (Royal 2 B VII, f. 25) dated to *c.*1310–20, servants and other non-combatants traveled with the army to set up their camp and take care of the soldiers while there. Spacious tents, such as these depicted were usually only for leaders. (British Library)

The battlefield of Campaldino from the tower of Poppi Castle. On the day of battle these agricultural fields would have been covered by thousands of Guelph and Ghibelline troops. (Authors' Collection)

initial advantages he may have, because he is subjected to a thousand perils'. Buonconte knew that the Guelphs outnumbered the Ghibellines two to one as for cavalry, and did not want to risk everything against very uncertain odds. A viable alternative would have been wearing down the Florentines and their allies by forcing them to engage in prolonged sieges of enemy fortresses, while having to keep watch for possible Ghibelline attacks against their possessions. Montefeltro's suggestion, however, enraged the Bishop, who had no intention of seeing his lands ravaged further. Turning angrily towards Buonconte, he snapped: 'You were never of that family!', implying that no true Montefeltro would show hesitation in the face of the enemy, and thus his interlocutor was not just a coward but also a bastard. Buonconte ignored the insult, answering with realistic fatalism: 'Should you come where I shall go, you will not return'.

The more experienced Ghibelline fighters shared Montefeltro's doubts, much to the scorn of their younger colleagues eager to come to grips with the enemy. One Aretine cavalryman by the name of Neri (the surname, unfortunately, unrecorded) is supposed to have exclaimed: 'Those who fear, should run off now'. To which an exiled Florentine knight replied with grim sarcasm: 'Neri, Neri you are still wet behind the ears because of your great youth. You will flee and I shall stay'. Benvenuto da Imola, an early commentator on the *Divine Comedy* who records this tale, adds: 'And so it came to be'.

The decision to fight taken, Bishop Ubertini sent the Guelphs a formal challenge, 'which the Florentines joyfully accepted', comments Villani. With their troops still streaming in, the Guelphs had reasons to be satisfied, since a set battle gave them all the necessary time to prepare themselves, and we can imagine their *marraiuoli* and *palaioli* being put to work filling ditches and levelling the ground in the same way as their Ghibelline counterparts. Having agreed to fight on the morrow, the two armies settled down for the night, eagerly expecting the inevitable clash.

BATTLE

On 11 June 1289, the day – both physically and metaphorically – began to get hot. Even at the relatively high altitude of the Casentino Mountains, as the sun rose so did the temperature. Haze caused by evaporating dew would have initially obscured the field, but it soon cleared revealing both forces, except for those few who had been hidden in reserve. Anyone looking north-west from the tower of Poppi Castle would have seen two huge armies facing each other across a field roughly 850m in length. They might not have been able to discern who was on horse and who on foot, let alone who fought under which seigniorial or urban banner, but they could only have been impressed by the huge numbers of men who were lined up on both sides between the Arno River and the *la strada del Casentino*, the 'Casentino Road'. On the ground, the men in those forces could see who was mounted and who was not, and they could have determined who fought for whom. Their awe at the sight, however, was tempered by their anticipation of what was soon to take place.

On the battlefield, the Ghibellines were deployed in four ranks. The first was small. Buonconte di Montefeltro had picked 12 skilled knights,

The church of Certomondo, built to celebrate the Ghibelline victory at Montaperti in 1260, played an important role in the battle of Campaldino. Count Guido di Guidi hid his reserve force in the unfinished cloister behind the church at the beginning of the battle, and it is from there that they retreated to Poppi Castle when he felt they could not come to the aid of the Ghibellines. (Authors' Collection)

Poppi Castle towers on the ridge above the battlefield of Campaldino, seen here from the position of the first and second Ghibelline lines on the day of battle. (Authors' Collection)

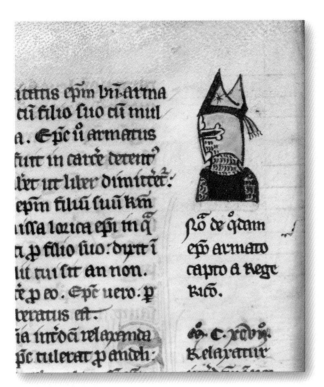

Although this image from the *Chronicon Roffensis* (BL Cotton Nero D II, f 121v) is of the bishop of Beauvais, it shows a clergyman dressed in mail armour, a mail coif and great helm. Atop his helmet is his episcopal mitre, showing his rank as a bishop. Although not seen in this illustration, his surcoat would have carried the same. At Campaldino, Bishop Guglielmino degli Ubertini of Arezzo would have most likely worn something very similar. (British Library, London, UK/© British Library Board. All Rights Reserved/Bridgeman Images)

dubbed the 'paladins', to act as a vanguard under his personal leadership. The creation of such task forces, and the name itself, was not unusual at the time. The second held another 300 cavalry; known at the time as *feditori*, literally the 'wound-givers' or 'strikers', these were the best of the Ghibelline cavalry, mounted warriors of strength, experience and physical prowess. How they were chosen among the Ghibellines is unknown, but they were probably selected according to both age and vigour. The third contained 350 more on horseback. And the fourth, led by the aged Bishop Guglielmino degli Ubertini, between 69 and 74 years old at the time, appears to have contained the entire Ghibelline infantry – as many as 8,000 strong. No more than 100 metres separated each rank. Another 150 cavalry were hidden in the unfinished cloister behind the Santissima Annunziata e di San Giovanni Battista Church of Certomondo. They were led by Count Guido Novello Guidi and could not be seen by the Guelphs. Hiding troops for a surprise attack is something Guidi had witnessed at Tagliacozzo in 1268, where the French used the tactic against the army he was fighting for. Somewhere among the ranks, their location unmentioned in the sources but possibly with the paladins, were Guglielmo Pazzi di Valdarno and his brother, Ranieri, Bishop Ubertini's nephews. High above the Ghibelline ranks fluttered the Imperial standard, bearing an eagle displayed sable on a field of gold and carried by the fiercely anti-Guelph Guidarello Filippeschi of Orvieto.

The military prowess of many Ghibellines equalled only the bitter hatred they reserved for their opponents. The most prominent Ghibellines of Florence, the Uberti family, had been exiled *en masse* from Florence after the establishment of the Guelph regime in 1267. Their houses were demolished, their property confiscated and their name publicly declared accursed, due to the perceived role played by Farinata degli Uberti in the Florentine defeat at Montaperti. Farinata's sons and nephews had spent nearly a quarter of a century nursing a burning resentment against their native city, being excluded from all amnesty decrees issued over the years in favour of other banished Ghibellines. Most were at Campaldino. Other Florentine exiles among the Ghibelline forces, such as Dante degli Abati, may have been less virulent in their anti-Florentine rage: Abati, after all, still had a lot of his Guelph kin left in the city and possibly hoped that family consciousness proved more powerful than any public decree. Still, he was determined on the field of Campaldino, as any other of his Ghibelline colleagues, to come to blows with his political enemies.

The Guelph army was deployed in three ranks. The first contained 150 cavalry, also called *feditori*. Florentine militia, they were nevertheless trained in fighting on horseback with couched lance and sword. Commanded by Vieri de' Cerchi, on the battlefield he chose 25 from each of the Florentine *sesti* among volunteers who wanted to fight in the vanguard. Dante was among these. Evidently not everyone was quick to desire this service, though, as from his own *sesto* Cerchi chose his son and nephew, which encouraged and 'shamed' others to come forward. According to Villani, the first rank was divided into three units, as was the second one. This second rank had the cavalry in the middle, between 1,200 and 1,300 according to Villani again, with infantry either side. The numbers of infantry are unknown, but were divided into squads of 3 (a spearman, a crossbowman, and a shield-bearer [*pavesaro*]). Compagni has about 1,000 cavalry in the second rank. In the final rank stood the infantry, numbering roughly 10,000. The wagons and carts that had accompanied the marching Guelph army were placed in a line behind this final rank, no doubt to keep the army from being attacked in the rear, but also to discourage flight: Villani explicitly says they were placed there to 'contain' (*ritenere*) the main body. These ranks were separated by more distance than the Ghibellines, but the second and third ranks were also thickened by more men in them. A reserve, of 150–200 horse, commanded by Corso Donati, was hidden behind a ridge off the left flank and to the rear of the rest of the Guelph army. Beholding the enemy array, Bishop Ubertini, who was 'short-sighted', asked, 'what are those walls?', thinking he saw a walled city in front of him. 'Enemy pavises', he was corrected.

Ready for the impending clash, the Florentine *feditori* must have been keenly aware of how much their lives and, especially, honour were at stake. Scions of city lineages, ancient and recent, were heavily represented in the vanguard, who, however, are nameless except for the Cerchi and Dante. Talano degli Adimari and his kin – rich, violent and haughty – were present, and probably one or more figured among the *feditori*. Also present were a number of the small but powerful Visdomini *consorteria*: Visdomini, Tosinghi and della Tosa, who enjoyed the Florentine bishopric's revenues when vacant, 'growing fat while sitting in consistory [the formal gathering of

It is near this point that the main Guelph infantry force was positioned at the battle of Campaldino. The Guelph second line was approximately 100m in front of them, making it a short distance for these infantry to charge to reinforce those troops as they stood against the charges of the Ghibellines. (Authors' Collection)

the diocese]', according to Dante's snide comment. Not in the vanguard, but holding the important position of *capitaneus peditum* (infantry commander), stood Gentile Buondelmonti, the murder of whose kinsman Buondelmonte in 1216 had been the ostensible cause of Florence being divided into Guelphs and Ghibellines.

The commanders of each side were experienced enough to know their strengths and weaknesses. One would have to be weighed against the other. The Ghibellines were skilled in military conflict, and some of the older men would have remembered the utter defeat of the Guelphs at Montaperti in 1260 – they, no doubt, had repeated the story so often to their younger comrades that those too revelled in that victory. The Church at Certomondo, which all could see just over the road to their right, was a sufficient reminder, as it had been built by one of their commanders, Count Guido Guidi as a thanksgiving for Montaperti, while another, Bishop Guiglielmino degli Ubertini, had consecrated it. Many of the Ghibellines would also have fought in their victory at Pieve al Toppo. They had also picked the battlefield, choosing terrain that their experienced cavalry could exploit. But their army was smaller than their opponents, even with the addition of the Lords of Romagna with their retinues and Orvieto volunteers to the larger Arentine forces.

The Guelphs had the numbers, especially as the Florentine urban forces had been joined by soldiers from Siena, Pistoia, Bologna, Lucca, Prato, the Romagna, San Miniato, San Gimigniano, Volterra, and other small towns, as well as exiled Arentine Guelphs. However, they had little experience and the memories of those two battles lost, which were inspiring the Ghibellines, also raised the worry that they might fail again. The only recent Guelph victory had been Colle Val d'Elsa in 1269, and this largely because of their French allies. To bolster their ranks and confidence, King Charles II of Naples had sent two important knights, Amauri of Narbonne and Guillaume de Durfort. Narbonne and Durfort were to take titular command over the Guelph army, although it is clear that local leaders, in particular Corso Donati, Vieri de' Cerchi, and Barone de Mangiadori, would give the orders which most would follow, especially the Florentine cavalry on whom so much military responsibility was placed. A Florentine was also to carry the royal banner during the battle, Gherardo de' Tornaquinci (known as *Ventraia*, that is 'belly'). Twenty more Florentine young men were dubbed knights on the field that morning. The Ghibellines also dubbed knights on the battlefield, although their number is not recorded.

The Ghibelline commanders planned to attack first, with cavalry. Only Buonconte and his paladins seem to have been put into this charging vanguard. But, why? How could only 12 win against the entire Guelph front line, all mostly cavalry? There is only one answer, one that seems almost suicidal to modern minds, but fits nicely into the bravado and tactical scheme of these knights. They were to be a lure to

A detail from Pietro Lorenzetti's *Crucifixion*, painted between 1316 and 1319, in the Lower Church of San Francesco in Assisi, shows two mounted soldiers holding spears and dressed in mail armour. Their mail coifs are tied into place over padded arming headpieces; great helms would sit on these with relative comfort. (Calvary (fresco), Lorenzetti, Pietro (c.1284–after 1345)/San Francesco, Lower Church, Assisi, Italy/ Bridgeman Images)

The Ghibelline battle plan

GUELPH FORCES
1. Florentine *feditori*; 150 knights and men-at-arms.
2. Infantry (pavesari, spearmen/staff-weapon holders, crossbowmen); roughly 600–800 men.
3. Main body of Guelph cavalry; 950–1,100 knights and men-at-arms in 4–5 ranks deep.
4. Infantry (pavesari, spearmen/staff-weapons, crossbowmen); roughly 3,000–3,500 men in multiple ranks.
5. Guelph baggage train with *villanata* infantry, sappers and miners, some horse; roughly 4,500–5,000 men.
6. Corso Donati's reserve cavalry and infantry; 200 knights and men-at-arms, plus roughly 500–600 light infantry.
7. Carts, to 'contain the Guelph forces.
8. Guelph camp.

GHIBELLINE FORCES
A. Guido Novello Guidi with 150 reserve Ghibelline cavalry and some infantry.
B. Ghibelline *feditori*; 300 knights and men-at-arms.
C. Main body of Ghibelline cavalry; 350 knights and men-at-arms.
D. Ghibelline infantry under Bishop Guglielmino degli Ubertini; 8,000 men.
E. Ghibelline paladins; 12 knights.

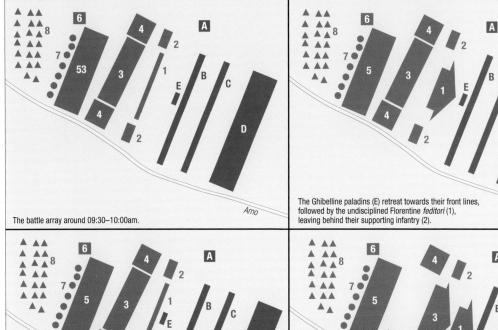

The battle array around 09:30–10:00am.

The Ghibelline paladins (E) retreat towards their front lines, followed by the undisciplined Florentine *feditori* (1), leaving behind their supporting infantry (2).

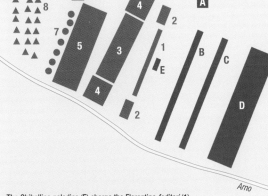

The Ghibelline paladins (E) charge the Florentine *feditori* (1).

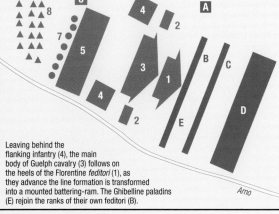

Leaving behind the flanking infantry (4), the main body of Guelph cavalry (3) follows on the heels of the Florentine *feditori* (1), as they advance the line formation is transformed into a mounted battering-ram. The Ghibelline paladins (E) rejoin the ranks of their own feditori (B).

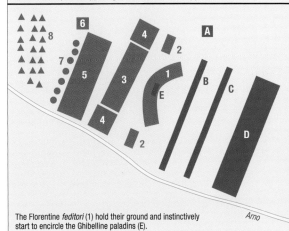

The Florentine *feditori* (1) hold their ground and instinctively start to encircle the Ghibelline paladins (E).

The Florentine *feditori* (1) and Guelph cavalry (3) hit the Ghibelline lines, pushing back the Ghibelline *feditori* (B) into their second line (C). Guido Novello Guidi (A) hits the Guelph left flank and rear with his reserve cavalry, as the Ghibellines (A, B) start to encircle their foes. The Ghibelline infantry (D) intervenes in support of the horse. Before the Guelph infantry (2, 4) is able to join the fray, the Ghibellines have annihilated their mounted opponents and can now turn their attention to the advancing enemy foot.

A fresco from the Palazzo Comunale, San Gimignano, attributed to Azzo di Masetto, *c.* 1290, showing two knights fighting with swords. (Photo by DeAgostini/Getty Images)

draw the Guelph cavalry to them, and, naturally, as there were only 12 of these paladins, they would be pushed back by the Guelphs into the main Ghibelline cavalry force. Buonconte must have known that Florentines, who made up about half the Guelph cavalry, would be in the front rank. He thought little of their military abilities, surmising that their incompetence would allow them to be lured forward easily in the face of a charge by such small numbers. The second Guelph line of cavalry would surely join in the fight, seeing their vanguard moving forward so impressively against this charge. Both sides' cavalry would then be embroiled in a mêlée – where the experience of the slightly outnumbered Ghibellines would give them the advantage – which is when the cavalry of Guido Guidi would rush from the cloister of the Church of Certomondo onto the Guelph rear. Ubertini's infantry could then also join the battle, their close position behind the first two lines enabling them to enter the fray quickly. By the time the Guelph infantry, much farther from the front line, had time to react it would be too late. The Ghibellines would have defeated the Guelph cavalry and be rushing onto the infantry. At this point, the remaining Guelphs would surely flee from the field rather than fight and victory would be had by the Ghibellines. The plan was a solid one and should certainly lead to victory. One has to marvel at the confidence displayed by these paladins, confidence both in their equanimity to accept a failure that would produce a Ghibelline success, and confidence that their skill at arms and armour would ward off blows that might lead to their deaths.

The Guelph plan was entirely different. Compagni has Barone de Mangiandori, an 'experienced and outspoken knight' – still alive when Compagni was writing, and perhaps his authority on the speech – announce to the gathered knights and cavalry: 'My lords, the wars in Tuscany once were won with vigorous attacks and did not last, and few people died because there was no tradition (*uso*) of killing. Now things have changed, and you win by standing very firmly. Thus I advise that you be strong, and let yourself be attacked'. They were convinced. Battle orations given by commanders of victorious armies are always convincing. In this case, it was the only advice that could bring victory. Were any of the Guelph lines to move from defensive formations – charging ahead against the 12 Ghibelline paladins, for example – they would be defeated by their much more experienced opponents. So, the plan was agreed to, by everyone, or almost everyone. Only Donati seems to have been wavering in his decision to adopt a defensive posture, or perhaps it was simply because he was prone to hot-headedness. He was pointedly told, likely by Narbonne or Durfort, 'on pain of death' (literally that he would lose his head), that he was not to move the reserve which he commanded until ordered to do so.

How might Narbonne or Durfort have given this command to Donati? A courier might have been sent – on horse or foot – but this was usually done only if a command contingent was left out of the fighting, which is not said to be the case at Campaldino. In the midst of the battle, finding a man to take the message to Donati, and then sending it, would have been difficult to undertake. A second possibility was using signal flags. Signal flags had been used since ancient times, but they could also easily be obscured on a hot day by dust and haze. A final way of sending command signals would be with musical instruments. The use of drums, horns, bagpipes and fifes would become commonplace in early modern and modern warfare. But were they also used in medieval conflicts, perhaps even at the battle of Campaldino? Dante provides solid evidence that they were. In an effort to demean the very loud fart used by a devil as a signal at the end of Canto XXI of the *Inferno*, Dante writes at the beginning of Canto XXII about the types of instruments he had heard used to signal commands in war against the Ghibellines: the *trombe* (trumpets); *campane* (bells); *tambura* (drums); and *cennamella* (reed

Two late 13th-century knights fighting each other with lances. From the Palazzo Comunale, San Gimignano, attributed to Azzo di Masetto, *c*.1290. (Photo by Fine Art Images/Heritage Images/Getty Images)

Large shields such as this, from the Bardini Collection in Florence, had been known in Italy since the 13th century, although this example dates to later. Typically, these large shields were used to protect crossbowmen and other troops from an opponents' missiles and blows during battle or sieges. They could be held by *pavesari* or propped up by wooden braces. At Campaldino the Guelphs may have set up a line of pavises in front of their front line to disrupt a Ghibelline charge. (Author's Collection)

instruments). The sounds these instruments produced were loud or shrill enough to pierce the extremely cacophonous din of battle. Undoubtedly, this is how Narbonne or Durfort would have ordered Donati to attack.

It is not known how early in the morning the two armies decided to put their plans into action. It was obviously a Ghibelline decision. The Guelphs, taking a defensive stance, had to wait until the Ghibellines made their battle-initiating charge. It was likely not too early, but also not too late. For the Ghibelline plan to work, the Guelphs had to deploy their ranks. Prayers would have been said – undoubtedly Bishop Ubertini led the prayers on the Ghibelline side – and a small breakfast eaten. But, as it was projected to be a hot day, the Ghibellines could not wait too long before initiating battle. Heat quickly affects well-armoured men, whose bodies become dehydrated and fatigued. Sunrise on 11 June 1289 was around 5:30am, and Villani claims that the fighting was over by lunchtime, between noon and 1:00pm. So, it is safe to assume that battle began no later than 9:00 or 10:00am and took two to four hours to be fought. Medieval battles were generally not lengthy, drawn-out affairs, and when they were, as at Hastings in 1066 or Mons-en-Pévèle in 1304, those writing on the battle indicate how unusually long it was. There is no such indication in the sources of Campaldino.

It may seem odd that pre-modern armies would allow each other sufficient time to prepare for a battle: in the case of Campaldino, that the Ghibellines would let the Guelphs arrive on the battlefield, rest and fully deploy their lines. Why did the Ghibellines not take advantage of the Guelphs, by swooping down on them and fighting against only a small part of the army as it marched out of the mountains? Battles fought before both sides deployed (ambushes for lack of a better term) were certainly known in the ancient and medieval world. The *Strategemata* (*Strategems*) of Sextus Julius Frontinus, written in the 1st century ad, gives historical examples of both good and bad ambushes, while Vegetius' 4th or 5th century AD manual, *De Re Militari* (*On Military Matters*), the most popular military 'how-to book' of the Middle Ages, provides straightforward instructions on how an army should set up an ambush, and how to avoid one. Medieval precedents had also been set for fighting only part of an army, with the rest arriving at the battlefield either during or after a battle was fought. However, the best 13th-century precedent, the battle of Bouvines (1214) – a battle well known throughout Europe – had the arriving Flemish army attack a French force without waiting for its Imperial or other Low Countries' components to reach the site of battle, rather than have the French army swoop down on this partial force of men. The Flemish leader, Count Ferrand of Portugal, would come quite quickly to regret this decision as first his troops were defeated and then those who had arrived and were still arriving. Ambushes as a form of warfare were generally treated with contempt in the pre-modern world, as being dishonourable or even unchivalric ('against the laws of war'). The famous *Song of Roland* is a perfect example of this disapproval, and Dante would echo this sentiment by stating that at Tagliacozzo the French had won due to cunning rather than weapons. Pieve al Toppo had also been

This illumination, from the Pierpont Morgan Picture Bible (formerly Maciejowski Psalter), made in France c.1250, depicts a battle outside a fortification. Despite the four decades, the arms and armour that both sides would have used at Campaldino are clearly depicted, including mail armours, great helms, kettle hats, conical helmets, swords, lances, daggers and staff weapons. (Alamy)

an ambush, and they would become more frequent in the early 14th century, as the number of battles increased markedly – for example, at Mortgarten (1314), Auberoche (1345) and Le Roche-Derrien (1347) – and by the 15th century were a well-practised, if not entirely accepted, form of conflict.

Honour and chivalry may have played a role in the Ghibelline leaders' decision to let the Guelphs fully deploy at Campaldino. But confidence in their soldiers' abilities and a desire to fell the Guelph forces with a single blow – to gain a decisive victory – were certainly the primary reasons. All were very experienced generals. Guidi, Montefeltro and Ubertini had all been in battles before (Montaperti in 1260, Tagliacozzo in 1268 and Colle Val d'Elsa in 1269 for Guidi; Pieve al Toppo in 1288 for Montafeltro; and Montaperti for Ubertini) – a rarity in this period when battles were few. Tagliacozzo and Colle Val d'Elsa were Ghibelline defeats; Montaperti and Pieve al Toppo victories. Bishop Ubertini had also directed a concerted campaign of warfare for more than two years, as well as other more isolated military activities throughout his entire episcopate. The Ghibelline leaders certainly knew how to wage war. These conflicts also meant that they could count on their men's military experience to make up for the deficiency in numbers. Villani calls them '*molto bella gente*' (very good men, read fighters), 'adroit', the 'flower of the Ghibellines of Tuscany', and the nearby regions, 'all very skilled in wielding weapons and in the practice of war' and 'willing to fight the [Guelphs] although outnumbered in knights two to one'. Because of this, Villani continues, they despised the Guelphs, whom they characterized as 'tart[ing] themselves as women and comb[ing] their long hair'. The Ghibellines were 'disgusted' by them, deeming them 'of no worth'.

With soldiers like these, the Ghibelline leaders reckoned, they could end the Guelph threat once and for all. So many men had been mustered by the

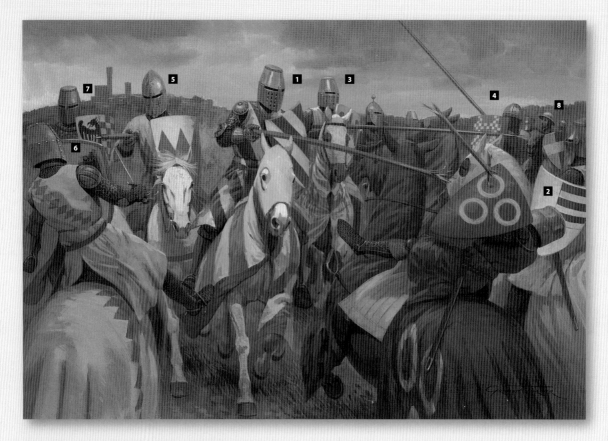

THE CHARGE OF THE PALADINS (PP. 60–61)

The scene pictures the stunning effect of the Ghibelline 12-man vanguard against the Florentine *feditori*, the experienced professionals smashing through the ranks of the amateur citizen warriors and sending them into headlong flight.

Buonconte di Montefeltro (1) unhorses Vieri de' Cerchi (2), the latter's bad leg hardly a help in keeping him on the saddle. Montefeltro is wearing state-of-the-art armour, including metal greaves, leather reinforcements on the upper arms and shoulders, iron gauntlets, plus a coat of plates hidden by his surcoat. Cerchi is similarly well equipped, his large fortune allowing him the most up to date armour, including the stylish decorated leather greaves. At his right, a knight of the Visdomini family sports a metal reinforcement on the front of the helmet, usually reserved for jousting but equally handy in battle.

To Buonconte's left, Count Buatto Schianteschi da Montedoglio (3) engages a member of the Falconieri family (4). Although an ancient lineage, at the time of Campaldino the Falconieri were no longer top-notch socially and financially, as reflected by the somewhat old-fashioned helmet worn by this individual. Still, he has seen fit to invest in a horse caparison to protect his modestly valued charger to some extent.

Guglielmo de' Pazzi di Valdarno (5) is about to slam into a member of the Bardi family (6), unfortunate enough to be tackled at the same time by a Florentine exile of the Uberti (7) – factional hatred giving extra force to the outcast's charge. Like Vieri de' Cerchi, Bardi's wealth as a banker can be fathomed by his fashionable armour. Pazzi is wearing the latest style sugar-loaf great helm and, like Buonconte, uses gauntlets to protect his hands, the upper arm defences hidden under the sleeves of his surcoat. Uberti had donned a riveted coat of plates of Aragonese origin, probably the result of one branch of the Uberti having taken up residence in Sicily.

At the far right the poet Dante Alighieri (8), the future author of the *Divine Comedy*, is about to turn tail and flee towards the Guelph second line, admitting later to have being smitten with *timenza molta*, 'great fear'. Undoubtedly many of his fellow *feditori* partaking of the same feeling.

Florentines of their militia – including all the cavalry – and so many from their allied cities' militias, that a victory at Campaldino would at the very least halt the current Guelph threat to Ghibelline holdings in Tuscany and neighbouring regions. Raiding into the others' territories had been conducted by both sides; Ghibellines had reached as far as the outskirts of Florence, while Guelphs had reached the gates of Arezzo and ransacked the upper Arno Valley. Because the Guelphs were more of an urban phenomenon, however, it meant that these raids had been comparatively much harder economically for the Ghibellines to bear. It was reasonable to anticipate that a defeat at Campaldino would cripple the Guelphs' military capabilities. Not only would raids against Ghibelline lands be fewer, but the opportunity to successfully occupy Guelph lands was worth the gamble on their soldiers' superiority over their enemies to Ubertini, Guidi and Pazzi di Valdarno.

A third reason for the Ghibelline leaders' decision must also be considered: they firmly believed that God was with them. How could He not be? Montaperti and Pieve al Toppo had proven God's favour. And they were led by a Bishop, one whom God had kept on the episcopal throne of Arezzo for more than four decades. Naturally, the Guelphs ostensibly counted among their supporters the bishop's boss, Pope Nicholas IV, so they felt that God was on their side, too.

The battle began. From the Ghibelline leaders came the cry that resounded throughout the ranks of their soldiers, 'San Donato cavaliere' (Saint Donatus the knight, or we are the knights of Saint Donatus – Saint Donatus is the patron saint of Arezzo). The Guelphs responded with 'Narbona cavaliere' (Narbonne the knight, or we are the knights of Narbonne). It was a mocking retort to the Ghibellines' invocation to a hallowed being; the Guelphs were saying that they were led by someone actually on the battlefield that day.

The savagery of a mêlée is well captured in this illumination dated c.1300. Mangled corpses, both human and animal, litter the ground with scattered limbs. In the centre, a severed head can be seen tumbling down. (Biblioteca Riccardiana, Firenze, *Sallustiano* 1538, f, 9v. Su concessione del Ministero dei Beni e delle Attività Culturali e del Turismo)

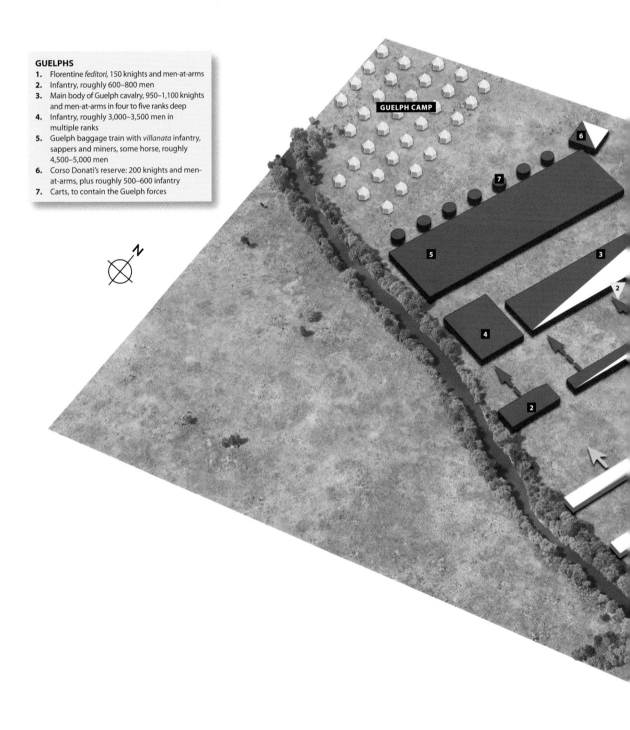

GUELPHS
1. Florentine *feditori*, 150 knights and men-at-arms
2. Infantry, roughly 600–800 men
3. Main body of Guelph cavalry, 950–1,100 knights and men-at-arms in four to five ranks deep
4. Infantry, roughly 3,000–3,500 men in multiple ranks
5. Guelph baggage train with *villanata* infantry, sappers and miners, some horse, roughly 4,500–5,000 men
6. Corso Donati's reserve: 200 knights and men-at-arms, plus roughly 500–600 infantry
7. Carts, to contain the Guelph forces

GUELPH CAMP

EVENTS

1 The Ghibelline paladins led by Buonconte di Montefeltro charge the Florentine *feditori*, hoping to lure them towards the main Ghibelline line.

2. Unexpectedly, instead of pushing back their attackers the Florentine *feditori* break, fleeing towards the main Guelph body with the paladins hot on their heels.

3. The now-isolated front-line Guelph infantry joins the rout of the Florentine *feditori*, retreating at the run towards the Guelph main body.

4. Beholding the shambles ahead, the Ghibelline *feditori* and main body of cavalry advance in support of the paladins, leaving the Ghibelline infantry behind.

THE OPENING STAGES

The Ghibellines launch their innovative plan of battle.

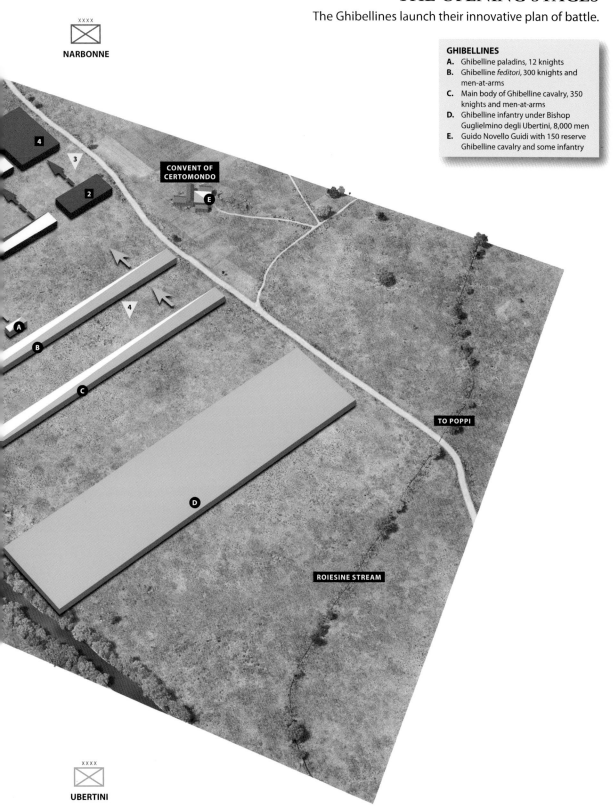

NARBONNE

CONVENT OF CERTOMONDO

TO POPPI

ROIESINE STREAM

UBERTINI

GHIBELLINES
A. Ghibelline paladins, 12 knights
B. Ghibelline *feditori*, 300 knights and men-at-arms
C. Main body of Ghibelline cavalry, 350 knights and men-at-arms
D. Ghibelline infantry under Bishop Guglielmino degli Ubertini, 8,000 men
E. Guido Novello Guidi with 150 reserve Ghibelline cavalry and some infantry

God and the numerous patron saints of the towns who had sent soldiers to the Guelph side were also sure to make their presence felt at Campaldino, so they need not be invoked; if they were not there, the Guelphs would certainly lose.

Then, as the Ghibellines had planned, the 12 paladins began their charge. Spurred on, their horses picked up speed. A medieval charge must have been awe-inspiring to watch, but terrifying to face. These paladins, all experienced, relatively young men from wealthy, aristocratic backgrounds, were undoubtedly outfitted in state-of-the-art armour and carried the most up-to-date weapons. While their warhorses were not tall nor big – medieval art of the period realistically depicted the straight legs of mounted knights descending below the horse's torso – they were sturdy and powerful. Both rider and horse would have heraldry prominently displayed, and these 12 knights' heraldry would be easily identified by the opposing soldiers they were targeting. Long, but not unwieldy lances would be levelled midway through the charge. Couched under the armpit of the knight, they protruded about two feet in front of the horse's head. When striking an opponent, they carried the momentum of the horse with them. An opposing soldier knew what such power transferred to such a small, sharp point could do. He would try to counter this thrust with his shield, but even if stopped or turned the lance-head, the blow had the force to break or deeply bruise the arm underneath it. Mail armour, and the leather or padded-felt underclothing, could also stop or turn a lance-head, but the wearer would certainly feel the shock on his skin and muscles, and the breaking of his bones. If the jugular vein, carotid artery or a major organ was hit, death could be almost instantaneous. If the skin was punctured or lacerated, it would take time for the wound to exsanguinate, perhaps enough time to have the bleeding stopped and the wound bound, but only if the soldier could remove himself from the fighting and get aid from one of the surgeons or his assistants who always accompanied medieval armies in war. Of course, should opposing cavalry be riding at each other, both had the impetus of their horses in lancing their opponents. But, if a rider was at rest, as the Guelph *feditori* were at Campaldino, they had none of their own impetus. The only thing

In this fresco from the Palazzo Comunale, San Gimignano, attributed to Azzo di Masetto, *c.*1290, a knight is smashed on the head by a blunt-edged weapon, perhaps a staff weapon or mace. (Author's Collection)

It was near here, on the banks of the Arno River, that the Guelph right flank was anchored. By the end of the battle, the shallow depression in the ground was one huge sanguine puddle, slowly descending towards the Arno, now red with the blood from fallen soldiers, giving image to Dante's 'river of boiling blood' in Canto XII of the Inferno. (Authors' Collection)

that kept them on their horses if hit were the high pommel and cantle of their saddle, and these, made of wood, could give way. No wonder Dante would express later his 'great fear' in experiencing the Ghibelline paladins' charge.

There was no more than 200 yards between the two vanguards, probably less, and that distance was covered in a matter of seconds. Still, it was sufficient time for the Guelph *feditori* to notice that only 12 were charging. Only 12? It is difficult to know what the Guelphs thought of the small number coming at them. Were they insulted? Were they amused? Did some perhaps think that they were being attacked by the apostles or Charlemagne's paladins? (The number 12 had great significance to a Northern Italian soldier.) They, of course, did not know of the Ghibelline plans – that they were not only to hold their lines but to push these knights back.

Instead, their rank was pushed back – even penetrated – as the paladins sailed clean through their line. 'They were valiant men at arms', says the pseudo-Brunetto *Cronica Fiorentina* (an anonymous contemporary Florentine chronicle once attributed to Brunetto Latini, one of Dante's teachers), adding that they 'fought more valiantly than ever had done the paladins of France', comparing these Italian warriors to those attested as the finest knights in the world at the time. The paladins punched through the front rank of the Guelph troops, with seeming ease. Many Guelphs were unhorsed, although no source claims they were killed. Chaos ensued as the Guelph front rank became completely disorganized and impotent.

Seeing this, the Ghibelline second rank charged forward into the fray, wanting to take advantage of what the paladins had initiated. The third rank followed quickly on their heels. Experienced should mean disciplined. But in military history it often does not. In these instances, those who should be disciplined are instead proud, and pride overwhelms wisdom, and instinct takes over. A lack of wisdom in military conflict does not always lead to defeat, but it almost always leads to ill-chosen decisions, which at the very least can turn carefully formed plans into chaotic and desperate situations. So it was with the Ghibellines at Campaldino.

At this very early point in the battle, the fact that the Ghibelline plan was in a shambles seemed of little concern. The Ghibelline cavalry was completely overwhelming the Guelph vanguard and by the time the second and third Ghibelline ranks of cavalry had joined the 12 knights who had

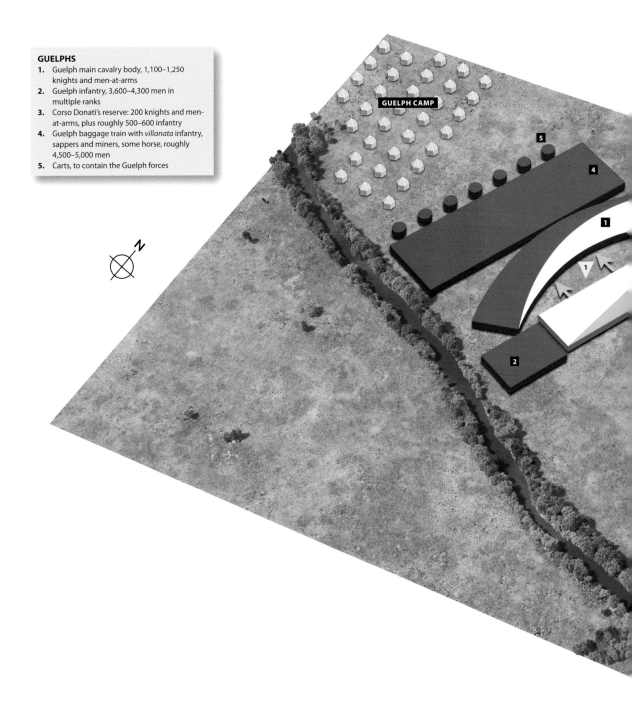

GUELPHS

1. Guelph main cavalry body, 1,100–1,250 knights and men-at-arms
2. Guelph infantry, 3,600–4,300 men in multiple ranks
3. Corso Donati's reserve: 200 knights and men-at-arms, plus roughly 500–600 infantry
4. Guelph baggage train with *villanata* infantry, sappers and miners, some horse, roughly 4,500–5,000 men
5. Carts, to contain the Guelph forces

GUELPH CAMP

▼ EVENTS

1. The Ghibelline cavalry slams into the main Guelph mounted formation, pushing it back 'a good bit' up to the rear echelon troops, but without managing to break the thick enemy formation.

2. Corso Donati at the head of the Guelph reserve strikes the Ghibelline right flank – on his own initiative, according to Villani.

3 In the meantime, the Guelph infantry starts closing the flanks of the enemy formation.

4. The Ghibelline's infantry, led by Bishop Ubertini, starts advancing down the plain at a pace.

5. The born survivor Count Guido Novello Guidi sees the writing on the wall before everyone else and begins retreating with his men towards the castle of Poppi.

THE GUELPHS RALLY

Pushed back by the Ghibelline cavalry, the Guelph forces rally.

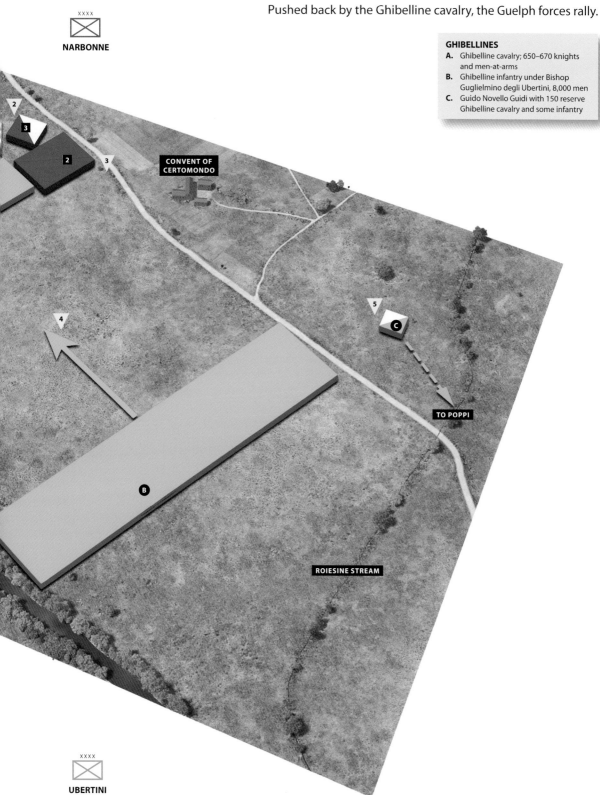

NARBONNE

UBERTINI

CONVENT OF CERTOMONDO

TO POPPI

ROIESINE STREAM

GHIBELLINES
A. Ghibelline cavalry; 650–670 knights and men-at-arms
B. Ghibelline infantry under Bishop Guglielmino degli Ubertini, 8,000 men
C. Guido Novello Guidi with 150 reserve Ghibelline cavalry and some infantry

In Nardo di Cione's *Last Judgement* (c.1350s) in the Florentine church of St. Maria Novella, Dante's vision of Hell is faithfully reproduced. In this case, the creators of discord dismembered by a devil's sword is a graphic rendition of what Dante himself witnessed in the aftermath of Campaldino. (Alamy)

so surprisingly and so thoroughly disrupted their direct opponents, probably in less than two minutes, the Guelph vanguard had folded. Those lucky to still be horsed rode towards their second rank; those unhorsed and the flanking infantry ran as fast they could.

All these troops now fell on the Guelph second rank, fleeing Guelphs as well as pursuing Ghibelline cavalry. The impact was substantial. Both Compagni and Villani insist that the Guelph rank recoiled from the blow – pushed back 'considerably', writes Compagni; 'a good amount', writes Villani. But both also have them ultimately holding rather than breaking. Villani describes them as 'not disrupted nor broken, but determined and strong' in their defence. Compagni agrees, although he notes that the Ghibellines penetrated quite far into, although not through, their opponents' mass of men and horses. As the Guelph cavalry began to find its footing, the infantry on the wings of this rank began to close in on the flanks of Ghibelline cavalry. The tide was beginning to turn.

Sometime after this occurred, the infantries in the final ranks of both armies charged forward to join in the mêlée. This could have simply been instinctive, seeing their comrades in arms needing aid in gaining victory or warding off defeat. They could also have been commanded to do so. Of course, by this time in the battle the Ghibelline plan had completely disintegrated. Instead of having their large force of infantry only around 100m from the mêlée and the Guelph infantry a much further distance away, as planned, the reverse had happened: the Ghibelline troops were more than 400m from the fighting, while the Guelph infantry was now less than 100m distant. The Guelph infantry could join the fighting in a relatively short time, while their Ghibelline counterparts would take much, much longer.

Another part of the Ghibelline plan had also become reversed. Count Guidi's reserve was supposed to rush into the mêlée as surprise reinforcements. But it was now completely out of his sight – even if he had spotters on the roof of the church, the battle was now taking place too far away. It was not, however, too far away for Donati to do what Guidi was supposed to. From his hiding place, Donati could see not only how the mêlée was faring, but also that the Ghibelline infantry was on the move to join in. Before they reached the fighting, Donati could make a difference. Yet, he had been threatened with death were he to enter the fighting before being ordered to do so. 'Let us attack the enemy cavalry before the infantry enter the fray', Leonardo Bruni records him as saying. Villani records the Florentine knight as far more defiant: 'if we lose I want to die in battle with my fellow citizens; if we win, whoever wants can come to Pistoia to take me.' (He knew that the latter was not likely to happen. If the Guelphs were victorious, as *Capitano del Popolo* in Pistoia, he knew that it would take a concerted effort to capture him, one that would need to be made by people whose victory he would have aided. And, if they were to lose and he was not killed in the fighting, it was likely that the Ghibellines would have sought his death more than the defeated Florentines.)

Donati's cavalry force charged forward, hitting the Ghibelline cavalry's right flank, according to Compagni and Villani – Bruni has him hit their rear, although this makes less sense than what is said in the earlier sources. They were not expecting it and it thrust them further into disarray. Villani says that this was the main cause for the Ghibelline cavalry breaking into flight; Bruni says that Donati's intervention won the battle; Compagni, who elsewhere in his chronicle professes a severe dislike of the man, has it but causing significant destruction. There is no doubt it greatly influenced the outcome.

According to Bruni, the Ghibelline horse were unable to flee, however, as their infantry were now either embroiled in the fighting or close enough to impede their flight. Crossbow bolts were being shot from both sides, 'raining' is the term Compagni uses; he also reports fewer crossbowmen among the Ghibellines. These bolts were especially effective against the 'uncovered (or vulnerable) [Ghibelline] flank'. Whether this was the still exposed right flank of the Ghibellines (on the left flank of the Guelphs) or the infantry following on behind cannot be determined.

No modern equivalent can match the fury and confusion of a pre-modern battle. The ability to stand apart from one's enemy and fire at him with guns distinctly changed the ways battle were fought. Only on rare occasions, as at Crécy in 1346 or Agincourt in 1415, did archery play a similar role in ancient or medieval fighting that guns would play even by the end of the 15th century. Almost all early battles were decided in the mêlée of hand-to-hand combat, fought by individuals who wielded sharp-edged weapons (swords, daggers, staff weapons, lances and spears) or blunt-force weapons (rocks, clubs, maces and hammers). All required combatants to stand in close proximity if not next to each other. The air became stifling; the temperature rose; blood flew; adrenaline ran out. Helmets, shields and armour only intensified these problems. They offered protection, even

Two scenes illustrating Stricker's epic poem on Charlemagne, painted *c*.1300, show the warrior Archbishop Turpin riding with other knights. He is dressed in mail as are the other knights and wears a great helm, similar to that of Charlemagne, although with a mitre affixed to the top. This depiction could easily be that of Bishop Ubertini at Campaldino, although he would have worn his heraldic colours rather than the red archiepiscopal robe worn by Turpin. (St. Gallen, Kantonsbibliothek, Vadianische Sammlung, VadSlg Ms. 302, II 35v)

against the fiercest of blows, but also impeded the wearer. A closed helmet, the Great Helm worn during this battle, was very protective of the head and face, but it impeded sight and breath; a helmet more open at the face might mean better vision and ventilation but made the face and head much more vulnerable. Shields covered the body well, but impeded free arm and hand movement and, on horseback, limited the grasping of reins. Going without a shield left a side of the body vulnerable. Armour protected body, limbs and head, but was heavy and hot, especially as mail had to be worn over leather or padded felt for the comfort and added protection of the wearer. Metal and leather plates, added more and more frequently at the end of the 13th and turn of the 14th century, increased the protection at vulnerable points such as shoulders, knees and legs, but also increased the weight and heat. Weapons of all types and weights seemed to become heavier and heavier as a battle raged on. In no time at all a soldier would become fatigued and dehydrated; the hearts, lungs and other organs soon gave out. Within minutes, too, the air became fetid with harsh odours: sweat; spilled blood; vacated bowels and bladders. Blood seeped into the ground until it could take no more and then flooded upwards, until some describe it as covering the feet or rising to the ankles. Add to this the blood of wounded and dead horses. 'A river of boiling blood' is how Dante, in Canto XII of the *Inferno*, refers to something similar to what he undoubtedly saw at Campaldino; in that Canto, while riding on the Centaur Nessus, he sees men in this river, some entirely submerged, others up to their ankles, as he had similarly witnessed while riding a horse across this battlefield strewn with the fallen.

That was if one stayed standing throughout the fighting. Being knocked off a horse or to the ground made a man very vulnerable. Weapons thrust down into him from above were more easily aimed and far more deadly than those swung at him from the side or above when standing. Wounds taken in the eyes, neck, armpits or groin were almost immediately fatal – cutting into vital arteries and organs – while swords, spears, staff weapons and daggers could more easily penetrate mail and even plates if stabbed into a victim kneeling or lying on the ground. Even if not struck while on the ground, the difficulty of arising from a prone position against the mob of people still standing might mean death by choking, suffocation or drowning. Accounts of battles often describe deaths without any obvious wounds, as at Agincourt with Edward, duke of York.

At Campaldino the mêlée was as other battles. Compagni notes the overcast sky, with a 'great dust' flying everywhere – it was a hot day and the fields seem to have been bare of crops, perhaps why the Ghibellines chose the site, one where their horses could operate on flat and even terrain. No doubt as it continued, it became more and more difficult to breathe. A fierce thunderstorm was to follow the battle. Ghibelline infantry snuck under Guelph horses and cut them open, although Compagni's words seem to indicate no negative judgment in reporting this – as if the spilling of the horses' intestines was simply another terrible activity of battle, at least this battle. He seems slightly more emotional when it comes to the actions of men against men – the test of Campaldino, as the test of all medieval battles, was on who would prove heroic and who faint-hearted. 'People who were considered brave were shown to be cowards, and people who no one knew about gained reputation', he writes. Singled out was Vieri de' Cerchi, who showed 'great valour', along with one of his sons, 'fighting by his side'.

In the long-lasting mêlée men fell on both sides, especially in the middle of the fray. It was there that Guillaume de Durfort was killed, the cause of his death unrecorded, despite people still believing to this day the document, forged as a joke in the 19th century by the historian Cesare Guasti, in which Durfort's demise is attributed to a crossbow bolt. His burial, in the Basilica della Santissima Annunziata back in Florence, included a memorial showing him in full armour, dashing at a gallop into battle, his sword raised, ready to

Another view of the battle's 'killing field'. It is here where the two armies primarily met, and where large numbers of Guelphs and Ghibellines fell before the latter, sensing defeat, fled from the field back towards Poppi Castle (in the distance) and along the Arno River (to the right). (Authors' Collection)

THE DEATH OF BISHOP UBERTINI (PP. 74–75)

The scene depicts Bishop Guglielmino degli Ubertini's last moments, as the Ghibelline line collapses under the pressure of Guelph superior numbers.

Bishop Ubertini, fittingly against the backdrop of the white crossed banner of the Imperial Vicar, is pulled from the saddle by a Florentine militiaman **(1)**. Ubertini displays in full his family's coat of arms, but wears a mitre on top of his helm to show his clerical-feudal status and holds a mace as a sign of authority. The infantryman pulling Ubertini off the saddle has the symbol of the Florentine Scala (Ladder) militia company painted on his cervelliere and, like the rest of the Guelph forces, has added a red cross to his garments as a field sign.

Guelph infantrymen close in to finish the bishop off, also keeping at bay the Florentine exile Ciante dei Fifanti **(2)**. The years spent as an outcast from his native city have had a negative impact on Fifanti's finances, since he sports very basic armour compared to other Ghibelline men-at-arms. He's also lost his horse. The crossbowman from Lucca is fully equipped with a short coat of mail, underpadding gambeson and a kettle helm. Despite the belief that crossbowmen always skulked behind pavises, it is clear they often engaged enemy troops in skirmishing fashion. In the background we see the Aretine knight Arrigo di Guillichino **(3)** attempting to come to Fifanti and the bishop's aid.

As he tries to protect his uncle Ubertini, Guglielmo de' Pazzi is attacked by a knight of the city of Pistoia and an Aretine exile of the Bostoli family **(4)**. The blue bend covered with fleur-de-lys on Bostoli's shield is a sign of political allegiance – Guelph in this case, very much as the black eagle for the Ghibellines. Behind them, the Imperial standard bearer Guidarello Filippeschi from Orvieto is struck down by a Florentine knight of the Buondelmonti family **(5)**. In the background, Buonconte di Montefeltro is on the point of joining the imminent Ghibelline rout **(6)**.

In the foreground, two Aretine Ghibellines of the Tarlati *masnada* have just gutted the horse belonging to a Gherardini from Florence **(7)**. The infantrymen are well equipped with coats-of-plate, long daggers and bucklers, while Gherardini sports just the minimum equipment required for cavalry service, his dead horse following suit. To their right, Guillaume de Durfort lies dead on the field **(8)**. Although reconstructions of Durfort invariably show him wearing a fleur-de-lys covered blue surcoat, the inventory of his possessions shows no garments of such a colour, the unfortunate Frenchman on formal occasions, including battles, opting for scarlet or green.

strike, his horse's heraldic caparison unfurled by its speed. Of course, this is a stretch; the Guelph cavalry did not charge at Campaldino, this French lord probably dying in hand-to-hand combat against other, more lucky or skilled opponents. The Guelphs recorded only two more cavalry deaths by name, Ticci de' Visdomini and Bindo Tosinghi, the latter dying of his wounds once he returned to Florence.

Bishop Ubertini was also killed in the mêlée. He seems to have had the opportunity to escape, but chose not to. Early in the fighting, Bruni claims, after the Ghibellini infantry he commanded had joined the mêlée, some of his lieutenants insisted that the bishop take himself from the battlefield to safety in his town and castle at Bibbiena. In response, he asks if he might also save the infantry. Impossible, is the answer: either the infantry by this time was too embroiled in the fighting, or it was hoped that by their intervention the Ghibelline cavalry might not be completely annihilated. 'In that case', Ubertini bravely retorted, 'may we share death, since I am the one who led them to peril, and I refuse to leave them now'. Returning to the fighting, he was killed some time after. His body would be found at the end of the battle, recognized by his heraldic surcoat and his mitre atop his Great Helm. His nephews, Guglielmo and Ranieri Pazzi di Valdarno, were also killed. Ubertini and Guglielmo were buried with dignity in the crypt of the Church of Certomondo, although without memorial. Ubertini's helmet and shield were taken back to Florence, the shield hung upside down in the

This depiction of Hector's corpse carried away from the battlefield and laid in rest, from the *Histoire ancienne jusquà César* was painted in the early 14th century in Naples. It is likely that the corpse of Guillaume de Durfort was given similar honour as he was carried from Campaldino by the Guelph troops. (British Library, Royal 20 D I, 114r)

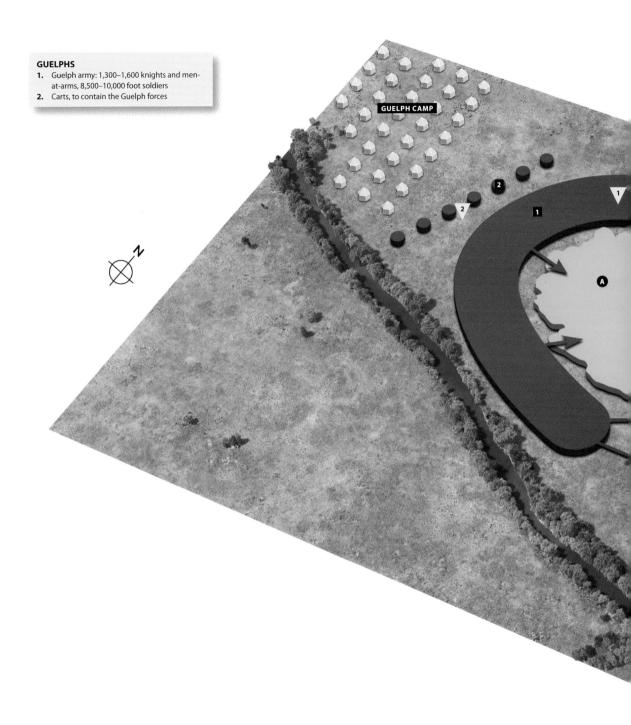

GUELPHS

1. Guelph army: 1,300–1,600 knights and men-at-arms, 8,500–10,000 foot soldiers
2. Carts, to contain the Guelph forces

GUELPH CAMP

 EVENTS

1 Donati's intervention and superior Guelph numbers disrupt the Ghibelline cavalry, who are now unable to retreat as they are compressed between the enemy and their own infantry.

2. The units guarding the Guelph baggage train join the fray, further bolstering the Guelph advantage in numbers.

3. The Guelph infantry closes in, compressing the Ghibellines and eroding their formation from the sides.

4. The intermingled Ghibelline horse and foot put up a brave fight, but by now are entrapped by the Guelph forces around them.

5. All Ghibelline resistance collapses into a chaotic mess, as the defeated soldiers flee for safety across the field in the direction of Poppi, pursued by the victorious Guelphs.

THE GHIBELLINE ROUT

Overwhelmed by superior numbers, the Ghibellines break and flee the field.

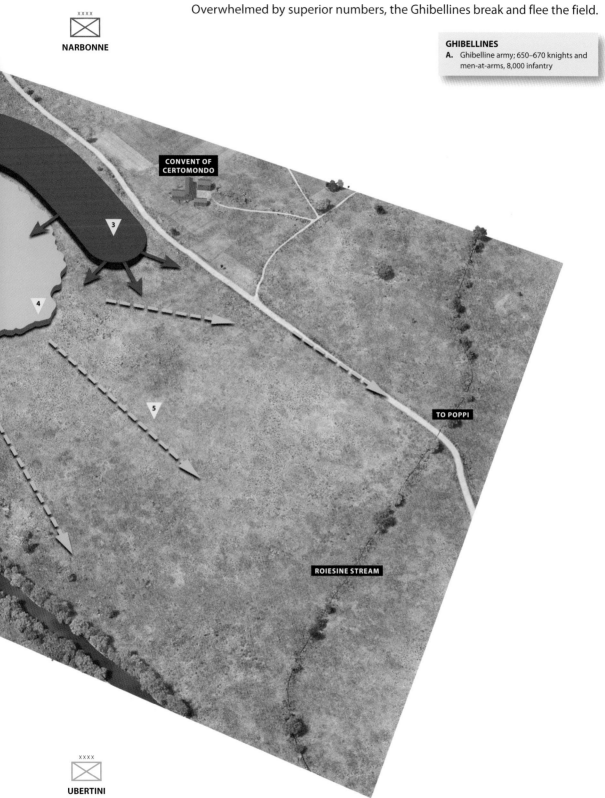

NARBONNE

GHIBELLINES

A. Ghibelline army; 650–670 knights and men-at-arms, 8,000 infantry

CONVENT OF CERTOMONDO

TO POPPI

ROIESINE STREAM

UBERTINI

The Arno River, taken from the dry bed of the Sova stream at the junction between the two water courses. The sight is similar to that on the early afternoon of 11 June 1289, the Arno at its low point and the Sova dry due to the dry season. The situation would change dramatically in the next hours, a sudden thunderstorm causing the Sova to flash-flood, carrying the bodies of those slain on its banks into the Arno. The vision of corpses carried downstream would inspire one of Dante's most celebrated passages in the *Divine Comedy*. (Authors' Collection)

Baptistery; the helmet was still there as late as 1460. With the bishop and Pazzi also fell Buatto, lord of Montedoglio, Armaleo, lord of Montenero, plus a number of Florentine exiles, including a score of the Uberti family, Dante degli Abati, Ciante Arrighi de' Fifanti and, the Pseudo-Brunetto reports, 'many other gentlemen whom in a century Tuscany had not seen the like'. Finally, Guidarello Filippeschi met his death in the fray, the Imperial banner he had once carried high now a trophy to be mocked by the victors.

At what point in the battle the victory was won by the Guelphs and lost by the Ghibellines cannot be known from the sources. How quickly is it before men decide to give up the fight and try to save themselves, or perhaps to push on, hoping that a battle might swing to their side's favour? At Campaldino, it seems, the battle was lost by the Ghibelline cavalry when they ranged too far from their planned 'killing ground' and thus distanced themselves too far from their infantry, although the final blow to any chance of victory might have come with the attack of Corso Donati's reserve cavalry. It is, after all, only after this assault that Bruni implies the Ghibelline cavalry tried to retreat, but could not pull back as their infantry arriving into the fray blocked the path. The rout would start later, after many more had been killed.

Long before this, however, it seems that Guido Novello Guidi from his vantage point at Certomondo, determined that a Ghibelline defeat was inevitable. Experienced in fighting battles over nearly 30 years, he both knew that his intervention, which would necessitate a charge far from where he and the other leaders had planned, would be fruitless, and that he should save those who rode with him, undoubtedly his own personal retinue. Moving slowly from the cloister, these soldiers climbed the hill back up to Poppi Castle, closing and locking the gates behind them, as well as those in the city walls. Guidi knew that his immediate duty was to his family and his men and he refused to risk them that day, even if it meant keeping out any refugees, former comrades in arms, who might seek safety among his fortifications.

This action was quickly branded as gross cowardice by the Guelphs, but it is hard seven centuries on to question Guidi's prudence. No Guidi nor Guidi retainer is recorded being killed at Campaldino. Although the battle dealt a devastating blow to the Ghibelline cause, it would live on in Tuscany in Count Guido Novello Guidi.

Once Poppi was cut off to those in flight, two routes remained. One led south-east around Poppi towards Bibbiena – the route suggested by Ubertini's men that the Bishop take earlier in the battle – and a second north to the Monastery of Camaldoli, sympathetic to the Ghibellines, and into the Montefeltro. This ran parallel to the branch of the Sova torrent. Refugees from the fighting fled along both these roads, hoping to make it to safety in some friendly abode. Bibbiena is 7km away, and the Monastery 13km away; Montefeltro was much further, around 82km distant, although once the Apennines were crossed into San Piero in Bagno, 40km away, and Montefeltro territory reached, the escapee was safe. There was no dishonour in running, Compagni writes, 'these were routed not because they were cowards or had fought timidly, but because outnumbered by the enemy'.

Not all the Guelphs who had fought at Campaldino pursued those fleeing from the battlefield. Many, especially the young Florentine cavalry, who

THE DEATH OF BUONCONTE DI MONTEFELTRO (PP. 82–83)

In this admittedly speculative, but completely possible, scene, Buonconte di Montefeltro's lifeless body **(1)** is discovered on the dry bed of the Sova stream by Dante Alighieri **(2)**, Cecco Angiolieri **(3)** and a knight of the Frescobaldi family **(4)**. Buonconte's fatal wound is evident from the spilt blood from the neck, streaking with crimson the soil below.

Dante has abandoned his charger for a more modest rouncey, the war-horse too valuable to be put in harm's way unnecessarily. Alighieri's armour follows the rules set out by Florence's militia laws, but nothing more. Likewise, his family coat-of arms is limited to an escutcheon sown on the surcoat; Dante, unlike his far richer companions, unable to afford a full heraldic display. The Florentine poet is shown pensive, as he beholds in pity his erstwhile foe.

The Sienese Angiolieri, however, has no such sentiments, mockingly waiving a *fica* (an obscene gesture of scorn) at the fallen Buonconte: payback for the defeat suffered by his fellow citizens at Pieve al Toppo and fitting for a poet whose main life interests were, by his own admission, gambling, drinking and womanizing. The wealthy Angiolieri is equipped with the best

the market can buy, including bone and iron gauntlets and a coat of plates, visible under the open surcoat, the neck protected by a collar studded with small iron plates. Being a committed spendthrift, he also has no concerns about putting his precious charger at risk.

Having lost his war-horse in battle, the Frescobaldi knight is riding an expensive palfrey, affordable for a member of the most prominent Florentine banking families, his wealth similarly revealed by the decorated leather protections on his arms and legs. Frescobaldi is seen drinking from a *fiasco* of *acquerello*: low-alcohol wine and a great thirst-quencher, obtained from crushing harvested grapes more than twice.

In the background two infantrymen **(5)** are seen dispatching the wounded and looting the dead. The one on the right, a city militiaman or a country levy, is protected only by a cervelliere and carries a targe with the emblem of the city of Florence. His companion on the left is better equipped, sporting also a mail coif. On his surcoat the blue lion rampant of Maghinardo Pagani da Susinana, thus revealing him to be a *masnadiere* of that Romagnol feudal lord.

had fought in the vanguard and centre of the second rank, were fatigued, hungry, thirsty and wounded. It was better for them to rest, eat, drink and nurse their wounds. Talano Adimari and his kinsmen decided they had done their duty and promptly returned to Florence. Others though, especially those who had seen little fighting, joined the pursuit – Compagni notes that there were several Guelph militia cavalry who 'stood there' and 'did nothing' during the battle. They did not even know that their side had won until the Ghibellines had fled from the field. These began to follow the Ghibellines in flight. Harassed by Guelph pursuers and peasant levies, those fleeing were treated mercilessly. The wounded, fatigued or just slow were hunted down. The peasants, Compagni reports, were especially vicious. Bodies soon lined both routes from the battlefield.

It is this retreat that inspired some of Dante's greatest poetic lines. Encountering Buonconte di Montefeltro in *Purgatorio* (Canto V), Dante seems not to recognize him – he may never have seen his opponent's face as it was probably covered by a helmet during the battle, nor does it seem that Montefeltro's body was found after the battle, although his death is reported by all sources. The Ghibelline leader approaches to tell Dante what happened to him:

> 'I am Buonconte, once of Montefeltro. / ... / I go among these souls with head bowed low.' / And I: 'What force or chance led you to stray / so far from Campaldino that your grave / remains to be discovered to this day?' / And he: 'There flows below the Casentino / a stream, the Archiano, which arises / above the hermitage in Appennino. /There where its name ends in the Arno's flood / I came, my throat pierced through, fleeing on foot / and staining all my course with my life's blood. / There my sight failed. There with a final moan / which was the name of Mary, speech went from me. / I fell, and there my body lay alone. / I speak the truth. O speak it in my name / to living men! God's angel took me up, / and Hell's cried out: Why do you steal my game? / ... / From Pratomango to the spine, he spread / a mist that filled the valley by day's end; /then turned the skies above it dark as lead. / The saturated air changed into rain / and down it crashed, flooding the rivulets / with which the sodden earth could not retain; / the rills merged into torrents, and a flood / swept irresistibly to the royal river. / The Archiana, raging froth and mud, / found my remains in their last frozen rest / just as its mouth, swept into the Arno, / and broke the cross I had formed upon my breast / in my last agony of pain and guilt. / Along its banks and down its bed it rolled me, / and then it bound and buried me in silt'.

Whether Dante was actually chasing after Montefeltro that day is not known. Compagni implies that the young Florentine cavalry, among whom was Dante, did not pursue the Ghibellines fleeing the battlefield. Yet, Dante describes a blood-stained course, which he surely saw, if not from Montefeltro then from others; so sometime before the deluge that would have washed the blood away, the poet rode away from the battlefield, following the route that had been taken by escapees, covered in the blood of the wounded. Montefeltro states that he is one of these. His neck had been pierced through, although he does not say by what. Some have suggested that this was a crossbow bolt, which surely could have done the damage. But, so too could a dagger, sword or spear. Whatever the weapon was, it had either penetrated the mail gorget which this knight would have worn to ward off such a blow, or it had found a space between where Montefeltro's gorget ended and his helmet began. Armour was made to protect as much of the body as it could, but there were always gaps, and those making attacks on armoured men knew where these might be.

Montefeltro was exsanguinating, bleeding-out, from this wound. Eventually he would die from a loss of blood – 'there my sight failed. There with a final moan … I fell, and there my body lay alone'. How long this took naturally depended on how severe the wound was. But Dante gives us a distance that provides some chronological framework as well. Montefeltro fell on the banks of the Archiano (Sova), where it meets the Arno River. These banks must have been clogged with the dead and wounded, unable to cross to the roads beyond that would lead them to the safety of the Camaldoli Monastery or the Apennine range. Perhaps they were heading towards fords in these rivers, made more numerous in the summertime heat. The storm thwarted their plans. Dante, once more surely a witness, recalls a 'dark as lead' sky, which brought a heavy rain. This rain was so intense that 'the sodden earth could not retain it', and a torrential flood followed. Montefeltro was already dead by this time, but his corpse was so close to the Sova that it would be carried into it by this flood, then to the Arno and away, never to have been found. The Ghibelline paladin leader had run and stumbled nearly a kilometre from where he was likely to have been 'pierced through'. He joined the roughly 1,700 of his comrades who also had been killed.

A number of Ghibellines were taken prisoner, 2,000 in total, according to the sources, and these were led back to camp, where it seems they were treated civilly by the Guelphs, at least according to the standards of the time. Several were freed in the next few days, 'some by ransom, and some from friendship'. The Sienese were especially insistent in letting some of the Ghibellines go free, one can surmise either as the same had been done for some of their citizens following the battle of Pieve al Toppo the year before, or because they did not want reprisals taken out against those still in Ghibelline custody. Eventually 843 would be led 'bound' to Florence. There some exiled Ghibelline Florentines who had been captured managed to escape. Most others, according to contemporary chronicler Paolino Pieri, died in prison. No one of prominent name is listed among these or other prisoners.

Also carried back to Florence and their allies' cities were the Guelph dead. These were militiamen, citizens, and they undoubtedly had loved ones awaiting the return of their sons, husbands and fathers. The hope was that they were alive; if not, they wanted their corpses to be buried in family plots or, at least, in nearby consecrated ground. Among these were Durfort, who was laid to rest with honour – a foreigner, but one who gave his life for Florence. Many were also wounded, on both sides. Dante describes seeing the effects of wounds caused by edged weapons in Canto XXVIII of the *Inferno*, 'the pierced flesh and severed body parts'.

The Ghibelline dead were also removed from the battlefield; many were to join their bishop at the Church of Certomondo in a burial mound north of the Church that can still be seen today. An archaeological survey of the mound showed that these had been carefully buried, singly, and not all together in a common grave. Ubertini wished to die with his men; he was also, at least initially, to be buried with them. (In 2008, his body was removed to the Cathedral in Arezzo.)

THE AFTERMATH

News of the victory at Campaldino reached Florence by courier at vespers on 11 June. However, the supernatural was always present in 13th-century daily lives and, according to Villani, the Florentines already knew about the battle's outcome. Soon after lunchtime, the priors had retired to their communal chamber in the city's government building for a well-deserved postprandial rest. Suddenly there came a loud knocking on the door, accompanied by the shout: 'Rise up, for the Aretines are defeated!'. The startled officials rushed to open, but, to their astonishment, nobody could be seen outside, their puzzlement compounded by the household servants' denial of seeing or hearing anything: 'This incident considered by all wonderful and notable' according to Villani, who adds 'And this is true, for I also saw and heard'. Once confirmed, the report of the Guelph success led to much rejoicing and celebration in Florence, the victory immediately attributed to the intercession of St Barnaby on whose feast it had happened. A church dedicated to the saint erected as a token of thanksgiving is still visible in Florence.

The view inside the church of Certomondo. Following the battle this small church, built initially to celebrate the Ghibelline victory over the Guelphs at Montaperti in 1260, became the resting place for many Ghibelline dead, including Bishop Ubertini, who was buried under the altar. (Authors' Collection)

Combining these metaphysical needs with more earthly ones, the Guelph army rested in camp the day after the battle. The wounded were tended, armour and weapons repaired, the dead buried and religious services held for the souls of the fallen. The Guelph army had enough carts to carry the now-naked bodies – stripping the lifeless was a customary practice in an economy of need – to the burial pits, something Dante must have witnessed. Indeed, an echo of those bare, mangled, rain-lashed, bloated corpses can be perceived in the poet's vision of the gluttons in the Canto VI of the *Inferno*.

Before long, however, the Guelphs were on the move again, their immediate objective securing the countryside. Poppi was considered too hard a nut to crack, but Bibbiena, devoid of defenders, was easily taken and immediately had its walls dismantled, the same fate befalling several lesser strongholds in the area. It took the victors eight days to reach Arezzo, to the chagrin of Compagni, who would later maintain that

The location of a mass grave outside the church of Certomondo, where the Ghibelline dead were buried following the battle. (Authors' Collection)

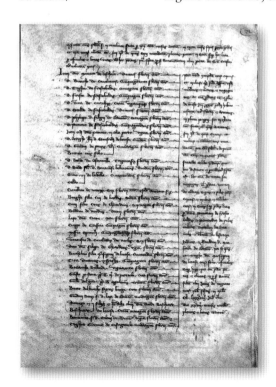

A list of horses lost by Florentine men-at-arms during the Campaldino campaign. Although the Commune of Florence had fixed a minimum of 20 and maximum of 70 florins for the value of war horses, in reality these parameters were wildly disregarded: the list includes a whopping 200 florins for Stoldo Frescobaldi's charger, to a mere 12 for Bindo Bellincioni's mount. (Archivio di Stato di Firenze, *Provvisioni*, II, f. 72r. Su concessione del Ministero dei Beni e delle Attività Culturali e del Turismo)

had the Guelphs advanced there immediately after the battle, the city would have fallen. This sort of wishful thinking was all too common among the politicians removed from the warzone and ill-equipped to understand the logistical and physical limitations of an army in the field. Once the Guelph forces reached the walls of Arezzo eight days later, the Florentine government sent two priors to supervise the siege operations – only to be curtly told by the soldiers there to mind their own business and leave military matters to professionals.

As it happened, the siege of Arezzo turned into a desultory affair. The Guelphs catapulted donkeys with mitres on their heads inside the city in mockery of the late bishop Ubertini, but the attacks against the walls, part of them but wooden staves, lacked the necessary vigour for a breakthrough. It could be argued that while the invaders still sought to impose a Guelph regime on Arezzo, the Florentine nobility was not too keen that it be run by the *popolo*. In any case, the Aretines showed sufficient fighting spirit not only to repel all assaults, but also to organize sorties resulting in the burning of siege towers. The Florentines at least had the satisfaction of running the *palio* under Arezzo's walls and occupying a number of strategic strongholds in the Aretine *contado*; so did the Sienese, besides retaking those fortresses lost after Pieve al Toppo. The siege was abandoned in mid-July, the focus of the anti-Ghibelline campaign shifting to the Pisan front, were Guido di Montefeltro had been causing serious headaches for the Guelphs. Indeed, for the next four years Montefeltro would do sterling work in restoring Pisan military and territorial power, taking Grosseto and the apparently impregnable Pontedera, threatening Volterra, San Miniato and Empoli, trying through conspiracy to topple the regime in Siena.

In the Appenines, the Ghibelline lords managed to create a united line of sorts across the mountain range and beyond, thanks also to Maghinardo da Susinana changing sides once again. Florence managed to contain this threat by a mixture of force and bribery. In any case, the Ghibelline defeat at Campaldino had forced Arezzo on the defensive, despite the new *podestà*

The Maastricht *Book of Hours* (c.1300) shows an ass about to be catapulted into the fortress by a counterweight trebuchet. This can be compared to the siege of Arezzo following the battle of Campaldino where mitre-crowned asses were mockingly catapulted into the city by the Guelphs. (British Library, London, UK/© British Library Board. All Rights Reserved/Bridgeman Images)

being Galasso di Montefeltro. Part of the problem was that the new Aretine bishop was of the opposite party, and thus they could count no longer on the human and material resources of the episcopal lands. In this respect at least, the victory at Campaldino had produced something positive for the Guelphs.

In Florence, the success on St Barnaby's day caused a renewal of factional fighting as the aristocracy, emboldened by their contribution to the victory, tried to push through policies favourable to them, often through physical violence. In 1293, a split within the ranks of the magnates allowed for a popular reaction, leading to the implementation of the Orders of Justice, which barred some 140 lineages from holding government executive positions or leadership roles within the guilds. The popular leadership was also keen to come to terms with the Ghibelline states and in July of the same year Florence and Pisa signed a peace treaty. No such agreement happened with Arezzo, although the rival cities managed to establish an unofficial and uneasy truce.

Although he did not fight at Campaldino, the Templar Guido Pallavicino's effigy, at the Cistercian abbey of San Bernardo in Fontevivo, shows important details of the armour and weapons of a major Italian knight of the period. Of special note are his distinct gauntlets crossed over his sword, sheathed and on a belt. His Templar robes cover an easily seen mail armour worn under a cloth-covered coat of plates. (Photo by Casalmaggiore Provincia/ CC BY-SA 4.0)

The Florentine aristocrats were, predictably, incensed by these developments: 'We are those who won at Campaldino and you have taken away from us the offices and dignities of our city!', shouted a group of magnates as they beat up some leading guildsmen on the feast of St John the Baptist in the year 1300. By then differences in foreign policy had caused the Florentine Guelphs to split into Blacks and Whites, headed respectively by leaders of Campaldino, Corso Donati and Vieri de' Cerchi. Two years later, covert French and Papal intervention allowed the Blacks to gain the upper hand, kicking their White opponents out of the city. Among the exiles figured a number of Campaldino veterans, including Dante Alighieri, who would maintain that Florence's and his own woes started on 11 June 1289.

Dante himself is the principal writer responsible for Campaldino's fame as a battle, due to its prominence in the fifth canto of Purgatory. Dante's popularity among 15th-century humanists only increased the clash's repute, to the point that the *literato* (celebrated humanist) Cristoforo Landino could write about the glorious deeds performed during the fight by a spurious ancestor serving within the ranks of the city militia. That Landino's father had moved his family from the Casentino to Florence only a few years before was conveniently forgotten.

Other memories, often bitter, lingered on among those directly or indirectly involved with the battle, as witnessed in one of his short stories by the Florentine writer Franco Sacchetti:

Not long ago two women were married into the family of the Counts Guidi; one was the daughter of Count Ugolino della Gherardesca, whom the Pisans had starved to death with his sons, and the other was the daughter of Buonconte di Montefeltro, a man who stood almost at the head of the Ghibelline party, and who (either he himself or some of his family) had been vanquished, together with the people of Arezzo, by the Florentines at Certomondo. Now it chanced that in the month of March these two women went out for a pleasure trip towards the Castle of Poppi. And when they reached the place at Certomondo where the Florentines had obtained their victory, the daughter of Count Ugolino turned to her companion and said: 'Oh, my lady, behold how fine is this wheat and these oats, here where the Ghibellines were overcome by the Florentines; I am certain that the earth still retains its fatness from that time'. She of Buonconte instantly replied: 'It is certainly fine; but we may die of hunger before it is ready to be eaten'.

The knight in the centre of the Gozzoburg fresco (*c.*1300) wears mail, which extends from coif to feet and covers his arms, although with separate, long mail gauntlets for his hands. Over the top of his torso he wears an additional armour, made of leather or quilted cloth, and over his lower waist and groin he wears metal plates seemingly affixed to an undergarment by rivets visible on the outside. Torso armour like this was becoming more common, but lower metal plates were rare, with few illustrations and no archaeological exemplars. Fashion may account for this, although with plate armours already beginning to appear in the late 13th and early 14th centuries, it is possible that this armour simply became 'old-fashioned'. (Photo by Wolfgang Sauber/ CC BY-SA 4.0)

THE BATTLEFIELD TODAY

The Campaldino battlefield is remarkably well preserved and rewarding, all the main features still recognizable at a glance. To reach it you will need a car and the trip on the SR70 taking roughly one and a half hours from Florence in good weather. There is the alternative of public transport, although it is between a 3½ to a 4½ hour bus ride to Poppi from Florence. Should you decide to go Ghibelline and start from Arezzo (for the Piero della Francesca buffs), the drive to Campaldino is about 50 minutes along the SR71, or one hour and 40 minutes by bus. Arriving by car from Florence the plain of Campaldino opens up in front of your eyes once you have passed the junction leading to the castle of Romena, a sight very similar to the one experienced by the Guelph army in June 1289. The church of Certomondo can be tricky to spot from the road, but should you park in front of the Caffetteria del Frate, the edifice will be right across the street.

The church of Certomondo stands on a rise and from there one can get a sense of how the Ghibellines were deployed, and also how the thundering cavalry under Guidi would have swept down the hill to hit the Guelph left flank, had things gone according to the Ghibelline plan. The church of

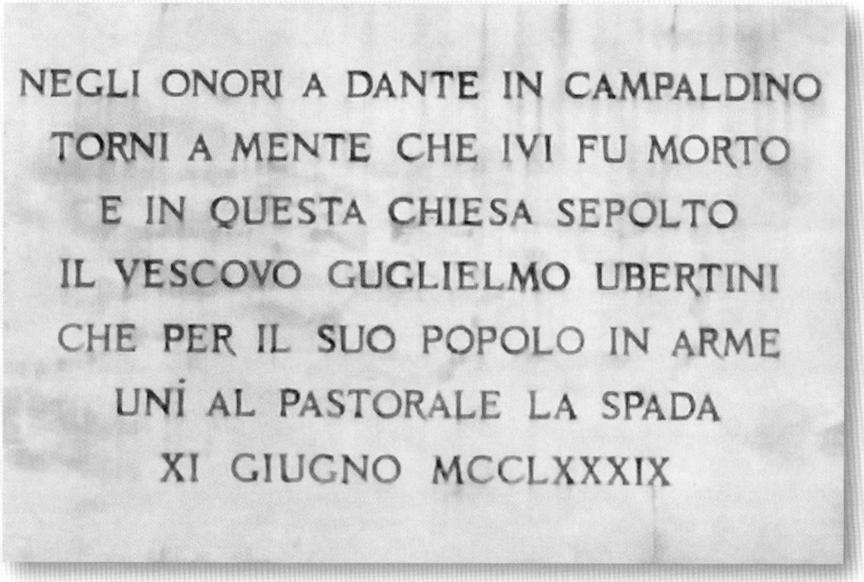

NEGLI ONORI A DANTE IN CAMPALDINO

TORNI A MENTE CHE IVI FU MORTO

E IN QUESTA CHIESA SEPOLTO

IL VESCOVO GUGLIELMO UBERTINI

CHE PER IL SUO POPOLO IN ARME

UNÌ AL PASTORALE LA SPADA

XI GIUGNO MCCLXXXIX

Inscription outside the church of Certomondo memorializing Dante's participation in the battle of Campaldino against Bishop Guglielmo Ubertini, buried inside (in 1988 removed to Arezzo Cathedral). (Authors' Collection)

This monument was erected in 1889 to commemorate Dante's participation in the battle of Campaldino. At the time it was thought that the battle was fought near this spot; however, evidence has shown it to be misplaced by at least a kilometre. (Authors' Collection)

Certomondo is usually closed, but, as often happens in Italy, luck may favour you with a bit of initiative and a few questions. When we asked the owner of the bar when it was possible to visit the church, he called the caretaker who lived upstairs and the doors were unlocked. Inside the church one can see the original grave of three Ghibelline leaders, while we received the extra privilege of beholding the plaster reconstruction of Bishop Ubertini's head, taken from his skull when the body was moved to Arezzo. On the right side of the edifice the risen terrain still bears witness of the burial pit for those slain in the battle, minus those like Buonconte di Montefeltro who – if you believe Dante – was washed away by the Arno River.

From the church, if you take a right along the main road, south and west of the farm Azienda Agricola San Marco, the ground starts to rise forming an easy slope. The Guelph main body was deployed beneath the ridge, the carts possibly on top to protect the camp and contain the troops. Further beyond, a depression in the terrain is probably the position of the Guelph reserve, hidden from the valley below. The land stretching out from the ridge is the 'killing ground', and it is possible to visualise Dante's description of a river of blood lying thickly on the ground.

The nearby castle of Poppi is a must, not just for the diorama of the battle (even if the reconstruction is somewhat questionable). The architecture of what was once Count Guidi's home is a very good example of how a 13th-century castle, really a fortified mansion, would have appeared. Climbing on top of the castle's tower one can see the whole battlefield and also understand Buonconte di Montefeltro's misgivings. Finally, after all the walking and climbing one can treat oneself to a *gelato* in the square beneath the castle, a more than pleasant relief if the weather is as hot as it was on the day of the battle.

FURTHER READING

Most of the sources on the age and battle of Campaldino are in Italian and in some cases – for example the medieval chronicles – difficult to read even for native speakers. We have tried to give as complete a bibliography as possible, with an eye for those not especially versed in the Italian idiom of any century.

Manuscripts

State Archive of Florence (Archivio di Stato di Firenze):
> *Provvisioni*, I–II

Signori, Dieci di Balia, Otto di Pratica: Missive, I–II

State Archive of Siena (Archivio di Stato di Siena):
> *Biccherna*, 99–106

Consiglio Generale: 35–39

Primary Sources

Alighieri, Dante, *The Divine Comedy*, Trans. John D. Sinclair, 3 vols, Oxford: Oxford University Press, 1939

Bartolomeo di Ser Gorello, *Cronica dei fatti d'Arezzo*. Ed. Arturo Bini and Giovanni Grazzini. In: *Rerum Italicarum Scriptores* (second series), XV.1 Bologna: Nicola Zanichelli, 1921, 161–336

Benvenuto de Imola. *Comentum super Dantis Aldigherii Comoediam*, Ed. James Philip Lacaita, Florence: G. Barbèra, 1887

Bruni, Leonardo, *History of the Florentine People, Vol. I: Books I–IV*. Ed. James Hankins, The I Tatti Renaissance Library. Cambridge: Harvard University Press, 2001

Compagni, Dino, *Dino Compagni's Chronicle of Florence*, Trans. Daniel E. Bornstein, Philadelphia: University of Pennsylvania Press, 1986

Dei, Andrea, *Cronica Sanese*, Ed. Ludovico Antonio Muratori, in *Rerum Italicarum Scriptores*, XV, Milan: Societatis Palatinae, 1729

Gherardi, Alessandro, ed., *Le consulte della repubblica Fiorentina dall'anno 1280 al 1298.* 2 vol, Florence: G.C. Sansoni, 1896–98

Manni, Domenico Maria, ed., *Cronichette antiche di vari scrittori del buon secolo della lingua toscana* Florence: Domenico Maria Manni, 1733

Paoli, Cesare, ed., *Il libro di Montaperti*, Florence: G.P. Viuesseux, 1889

Pieri, Paolino, *Cronica di Paolino Pieri Fiorentino delle cose d'Italia dall'anno 1080 fino all'anno 1305*, Rome: Giovanni Zempel, 1755

Sacchetti, Franco, *Tales From Sacchetti*, Trans. Mary G. Steegmann, London: J.M. Dent and Co., 1908

Schiaffini, Alfredo, ed., *Testi fiorentini del Dugento e dei primi del Trecento*, Florence: G.C. Sansoni, 1954

Storia della guerra di Semifonte scritta da messer Pace da Certaldo e cronichetta di Neri degli Strinati, Florence: Stamperia Imperiale, 1753

Tizio, Sigismondo. Historiae Senenses. Ed. Petra Pertici. Vol. 1, Book 2, Rome: Istituto Storico Italiano,1975

Villani, Giovanni. *Villani's Chronicle Being Selections from the First Nine Books of the Croniche Fiorentine*, Ed. Philip H. Wicksteed, Trans. Rose E. Selfe, London: Archibald Constable and Co., 1906

Secondary Sources

Battaglia di Campaldino e la società toscana del '200, La. Atti del convegno per il VII centenario della battaglia, 1989. Tavarnelle Val di Pesa: Graficadue, 1994

Battaglia di Campaldino, La: 11 giugno 1289, 2nd ed. Florence: Scramasax, 2007

Barlozzetti, Ugo and M. Giuliani, ed., *I settecento anni delle «giostre della Pieve al Toppo»*, Arezzo: Grafiche Diali, 1988

Bayley, C.C., *War and Society in Renaissance Florence: The* De Militia *of Leonardo Bruni*, Toronto: University of Toronto Press, 1961

Bini, A., '*Arezzo ai tempi di Dante (1289–1308),'* Atti e memorie dell'Accademia Petrarca di lettere, arti e scienze*, n.s. 2 (1922), 1–58

Boccia, Lionello Giorgio and Mario Scalini, ed., *Guerre e assoldati in Toscana, 1260–1364*, Florence: Museo Stibbert, 1982

Canaccini, Federico, *Campaldino, 11 giugno 1289*, Trans. Francesca J. Mapelli, Terni: Umbriagraf, 2006

Canaccini, Federico, *Ghibellini e ghibellinismo in Toscana. Da Montaperti a Campaldino,1260–89*, Rome: Istituto Storico Italiano per il Medio Evo, 2009

Canaccini, Federico, ed., *La lunga storia di una stirpe comitale: I conti Guidi tra Romagna e Toscana*, Atti del Convegno di studi (Modigliana – Poppi, 28–31 agosto 2003), Florence: Olschki, 2009

Cardini, F. and M. Tangheroni, ed., *Guerra e guerrieri nella Toscana medievale*. Florence: Edifir, 1990

I ceti dirigenti dell'età comunale nei secoli XII e XIII. Atti del II Convegno, Firenze 14–16 dicembre 1979. Pisa: Pacini, 1982

Chabot, Isabelle, 'Da Iacobus de Casentino alla famiglia Landini: decostruzione di una tradizione genealogica.' In: *Iacopo del Casentino e la pittura a Pratovecchio nel secolo di Giotto*. Florence: Ragazzini, 2014, 59–71

Davidsohn, Robert. *Geschichte von Florenz*. Vol. 2, part 2. 1908; rpt. Florence: Sansoni, 1957

Gasparri, Stefano. *I milites cittadini. Studi sulla cavalleria in Italia*. Rome: Istituto Palazzo Borromini, 1992

Hollander, Robert. 'Dante on Horseback? (*Inferno* XII, 93–126),' *Italica* 61 (1984), 287–96

Koenig, J. *Il 'popolo' dell'Italia del Nord nel XIII secolo*. Bologna: Il Mulino, 1986

Lansing, Carol. *The Florentine Magnates: Lineage and Faction in a Medieval Commune*. Princeton: Princeton University Press, 1991

Najemy, John M. *A History of Florence, 1200–1575*. Oxford: Blackwell, 2008

Oerter, Herbert L. 'Campaldino, 1289,' *Speculum* 43 (1968), 429–50

Ottokar, Nicola. *Il comune di Firenze alla fine del Dugento*. Florence: Vallecchi, 1926.

Paoli, C. 'Le Cavallate fiorentine nei secoli XIII e XIV', *Archivio Storico Italiano*, 3rd ser. 1 (1865), 53–90

Il sabato di S. Barnaba: La battaglia di Campaldino, 11 giugno 1289–1989. Milan: Electa, 1989

Salvemini, Gaetano. 'Florence in the Time of Dante,' *Speculum* 9 (1936), 317–26

Scharf, Gian Paolo G. 'Vescovo e signore: La parabola di Guglielmino degli Ubertini ad Arezzo (1248–1288),' *Società e storia* 138 (2012), 699–728

Settia, Aldo A. *Comuni in guerra: Armi ed eserciti nell'Italia delle città*. Bologna: Cooperativa Libraria Universitaria Editrice, 1993

Tabacco, Giovanni, 'Nobiltà e potera ad Arezzo in età medievale,' *Studi Medievali*, 3rd ser., 15 (1974), 1–24

Taucci, Raffaele, 'Guglielmo di Durfort e la battaglia di Campaldino', *Studi Storici O.S.M.* 1 (1933), 93–108

Tricomi, F., 'L'«exercitus» di Siena in età novesca, 1287–1355', in *Bullettino Senese di Storia Patria*, 112 (2005), 9–246.

Waley, Daniel P., 'The Army of the Florentine Republic from the Twelfth to the Fourteenth Century.' in *Florentine Studies: Politics and Society in Renaissance Florence*, ed. N. Rubinstein, Evanston: Northwestern University Press, 1968, pp. 70–108